The Reality of Man

The Reality of Man

Excerpts from the Writings of
Bahá'u'lláh and 'Abdu'l-Bahá

COMPILED BY

Terry Cassiday, Christopher J. Martin,
and Bahhaj Taherzadeh

Bahá'í
PUBLISHING

Wilmette, Illinois

415 Linden Avenue, Wilmette, Illinois 60091-2844
Copyright © by the National Spiritual Assembly
of the Bahá'ís of the United States
All rights reserved. Published 2005
Printed in the United States of America ∞

08 07 06 05   1 2 3 4

Cataloging-in-Publication Data
Bahá'u'lláh, 1817–1892.
     [Selections. English. 2005]
     The reality of man / compiled by Terry Cassiday,
Christopher J. Martin, and Bahhaj Taherzadeh.
          p. cm.
     Includes bibliographical references and index.
     ISBN 1-931847-17-7
          1. Bahai Faith—Doctrines. I. 'Abdu'l-Bahá, 1844–1921.
Selections. English. 2005. II. Cassiday, Terry. III. Martin,
Christopher, 1975– IV. Taherzadeh, Bahhaj. V. Title.

BP360.B2883 2005
297.9'3822—dc22

                                        2005041249

Cover design by Robert A. Reddy
Book design by Patrick J. Falso

Contents

Introduction

During times of turmoil we often witness scenes of unforgettable heroism as well as acts of unimaginable cruelty. At such times we may find ourselves pondering the true nature of humanity and wondering about our purpose here on earth. We may wonder about our individual destiny as well as that of our families, our neighbors, our friends, and others. Such questions may lead us to ponder other deeper questions. Where did we come from? What is the purpose of human existence? What happens when we die? Is there life after death, and if so, what form does it take? Do we have a specific role, a mission, that has been preordained for our life, or are the events in our life merely a matter of chance? Are we responsible for the suffering we experience, or is it beyond our control? Does God exist, and if so, what kind of a God is He, and why does He allow human suffering? Or is He merely a figment of our imagination—an illusion we turn to for comfort?

Our lives are constantly being pushed and pulled by so many external forces that we rarely find the time or motivation to explore such fundamental and challenging questions. If we are not busy working to pay the bills and keep up with the Joneses, we are probably busy trying to escape the pressures of paying the bills and keeping up with the Joneses, and little energy is leftover for thinking about such ambitious subjects. We are so swept up with the practicalities of daily existence that our search for answers to life's deeper questions may be postponed indefinitely. Daily struggles distract us from attempting to find any real answers to our deepest questions.

Religion—which is supposed to provide answers to life's most important questions—should, in theory, be able to tell us about God and human nature as well as provide comfort and sanctuary during the tests and trials that afflict us in life. And yet religion is often the source of even more questions.

Are some religions true and others false? Are all of them from God? And why do they seem to disagree so much? Is there, as some would insist, only one path to God and happiness? Perhaps we sense that the true essence of religion has somehow been lost in our materialistic world and that humanity as a whole has turned away from the teachings of religion. What, we may ask, is true religion, and how can it help us?

Bahá'u'lláh (1817–92), the Prophet and Founder of the Bahá'í Faith, understood the healing power of the written word and bequeathed to humanity a large body of scripture that illumines life's deepest questions. His writings offer a new perspective that contrasts with the harsh, judgmental view of humanity found in some religious circles. He explains that we are essentially spiritual beings having a material experience. Our purpose on earth is fundamentally spiritual, and each one of us has a unique role during our time here. But because we are constantly exposed to a way of life that emphasizes material success over spiritual development, we are often led away from ourselves and kept from discovering our true identity and path in life. We may feel disconnected from ourselves because the forces around us have distracted us, effectively blocking our spiritual connection to God. With this connection obstructed, we may turn away from God, convinced that He is not there or that He is not listening to us. When this happens, we feel depressed, empty, and alone.

The solution, Bahá'u'lláh tells us, is to return to the essence of what the Founders of every great religion have taught. Bahá'u'lláh proclaims that all religions come from God and are therefore sacred. He asserts that a loving God has periodically revealed

Himself and His will for humanity through different Messengers throughout history. His writings repeatedly praise and glorify these various Messengers of God—including Moses, Jesus, Buddha, Muḥammad, and others—as well as the scriptures of the different religions such as the Torah, the Gospel, and the Koran. By returning to the essential teachings of the Messengers of God, Bahá'u'lláh explains, we can get in touch with our true nature and with our Creator, and we can find our path to true happiness in life.

In addition to writing about the spiritual nature of human beings, Bahá'u'lláh also writes about the nature of God, telling us what kind of God is watching over us. He assures us that God created us because He loves us and that God wants us to love Him. Bahá'u'lláh states that the purpose of our creation is to know and to love God; by learning to know and love Him, we attain our true potential as human beings. We can also face our challenges in life with greater courage and resilience. The sufferings we encounter in life are often tests from God that help us grow stronger, to realize our spiritual destiny. Although God is just, He is loving, and Bahá'u'lláh assures us again and again that God's mercy and love for us are greater than His justice. God is always close to us and ready to support us, Bahá'u'lláh affirms, regardless of how often we may turn away from Him.

Although much of humanity may have lost track of God, God has not lost track of humanity. The role of Bahá'u'lláh, as God's latest Messenger, is to bring God's message to humanity once again to address the struggles and questions that trouble the world today. In this compilation, some extracts from the writings of Bahá'u'lláh are given along with some extracts from the writings and utterances of His son, 'Abdu'l-Bahá, whom Bahá'u'lláh appointed as His successor and the interpreter of His writings. The passages included here discuss the nature of God's relationship to humanity and why He created us. They emphasize God's love for humanity and how God shows this love to us. They discuss the spiritual reality of human beings, the nature of the human soul, and the progress of the human soul in this world as well as hereafter. They mention the nature of this world, our beginning in it, and what we can hope to achieve and expect both in this world and in the world beyond.

This book is for those who seek answers to the questions that philosophers, scholars, and religious teachers have pondered for ages. It gives a small sampling of the countless profound gems of wisdom available to those who delve into the scriptures of the Bahá'í Faith. The reader will find here a message of encouragement, hope, and a deeper understanding of who we are and why we are here. It is hoped that this healing message will not only provide solace and satisfaction for the reader who longs to find answers to some of life's deepest, most fundamental questions but also will motivate those who seek such answers to dive into the vast ocean of Bahá'í scripture to see what other pearls of wisdom might be found there.

God's Love for
Humanity:
The Generating Impulse

1

O SON OF MAN!

Veiled in My immemorial being and in the ancient eternity of My essence, I knew My love for thee; therefore I created thee, have engraved on thee Mine image and revealed to thee My beauty.

2

O SON OF MAN!

I loved thy creation, hence I created thee. Wherefore, do thou love Me, that I may name thy name and fill thy soul with the spirit of life.

3

O SON OF THE WONDROUS VISION!

I have breathed within thee a breath of My own Spirit, that thou mayest be My lover. Why hast thou forsaken Me and sought a beloved other than Me?

4

O SON OF BEING!

Love Me, that I may love thee. If thou lovest Me not, My love can in no wise reach thee. Know this, O servant.

Relationship with God: Our Purpose in Life

5

All praise and glory be to God Who, through the power of His might, hath delivered His creation from the nakedness of non-existence, and clothed it with the mantle of life. From among all created things He hath singled out for His special favor the pure, the gem-like reality of man, and invested it with a unique capacity of knowing Him and of reflecting the greatness of His glory.

6

*T*he purpose of God in creating man hath been, and will ever be, to enable him to know his Creator and to attain His Presence. To this most excellent aim, this supreme objective, all the heavenly Books and the divinely-revealed and weighty Scriptures unequivocally bear witness.

7

Having created the world and all that liveth and moveth therein, He, through the direct operation of His unconstrained and sovereign Will, chose to confer upon man the unique distinction and capacity to know Him and to love Him—a capacity that must needs be regarded as the generating impulse and the primary purpose underlying the whole of creation. . . . Upon the inmost reality of each and every created thing He hath shed the light of one of His names, and made it a recipient of the glory of one of His attributes. Upon the reality of man, however, He hath focused the radiance of all of His names and attributes, and made it a mirror of His own Self. Alone of all created things man hath been singled out for so great a favor, so enduring a bounty.

8

PRAYER

I bear witness, O my God, that Thou hast created me to know Thee and to worship Thee. I testify, at this moment, to my powerlessness and to Thy might, to my poverty and to Thy wealth.

There is none other God but Thee, the Help in Peril, the Self-Subsisting.

Our Spiritual Reality

9

Know, verily, that the soul is a sign of God, a heavenly gem whose reality the most learned of men hath failed to grasp, and whose mystery no mind, however acute, can ever hope to unravel. It is the first among all created things to declare the excellence of its Creator, the first to recognize His glory, to cleave to His truth, and to bow down in adoration before Him. If it be faithful to God, it will reflect His light, and will, eventually, return unto Him. If it fail, however, in its allegiance to its Creator, it will become a victim to self and passion, and will, in the end, sink in their depths.

10

Verily I say, the human soul is, in its essence, one of the signs of God, a mystery among His mysteries. It is one of the mighty signs of the Almighty, the harbinger that proclaimeth the reality of all the worlds of God. Within it lieth concealed that which the world is now utterly incapable of apprehending.

11

*M*an—the true man—is soul, not body; though physically man belongs to the animal kingdom, yet his soul lifts him above the rest of creation. Behold how the light of the sun illuminates the world of matter: even so doth the Divine Light shed its rays in the kingdom of the soul. The soul it is which makes the human creature a celestial entity!

By the power of the Holy Spirit, working through his soul, man is able to perceive the Divine reality of things. All great works of art and science are witnesses to this power of the Spirit.

The same Spirit gives Eternal Life.

12

*T*he reality of man is his thought, not his material body. The thought force and the animal force are partners. Although man is part of the animal creation, he possesses a power of thought superior to all other created beings.

The Nature of the Soul

13

*K*now that the soul which is common to all men cometh forth following the commingling of things and after their maturation, as thou dost observe in the germ: once it hath developed to its predestined stage, God manifesteth the soul that was latent within it. Thy Lord, verily, doeth what He willeth and ordaineth what He pleaseth.

As to the soul which is intended, in truth it hath been called forth by the Word of God and is such that, if it be kindled with the fire of the love of its Lord, neither the waters of opposition nor the oceans of the world can quench its flame. That soul is indeed a fire ablaze in the tree of man which proclaimeth: "No God is there but Him!" Whosoever hearkeneth unto its call is verily of those who have attained unto Him. And when it casteth off its earthly frame, God shall raise it up again in the most excellent of forms and cause it to enter a sublime paradise. Thy Lord, of a certainty, hath power over all things.

Know, furthermore, that the life of man proceedeth from the spirit, and the spirit turneth to wheresoever the soul directeth it. Ponder upon that which We have revealed unto thee that thou mayest recognize the Soul of God which hath appeared above the Dayspring of bounty invested with manifest sovereignty.

Know also that the soul is endowed with two wings: should it soar in the atmosphere of love and contentment, then it will be related to the All-Merciful. And should it fly in the atmosphere of self and desire, then it will pertain to the Evil One; may God shield and protect us and protect you therefrom, O ye who perceive! Should the soul become ignited with the fire of the love of God, it is called benevolent and pleasing unto God, but should it be consumed with the fire of passion, it is known as the concupiscent soul.

14

*C*onsider the rational faculty with which God
hath endowed the essence of man. Examine thine
own self, and behold how thy motion and stillness,
thy will and purpose, thy sight and hearing, thy sense
of smell and power of speech, and whatever else is
related to, or transcendeth, thy physical senses or
spiritual perceptions, all proceed from, and owe their
existence to, this same faculty. So closely are they
related unto it, that if in less than the twinkling of an
eye its relationship to the human body be severed,
each and every one of these senses will cease
immediately to exercise its function, and will be
deprived of the power to manifest the evidences of
its activity. It is indubitably clear and evident that
each of these afore-mentioned instruments has
depended, and will ever continue to depend, for its
proper functioning on this rational faculty, which

should be regarded as a sign of the revelation of Him Who is the sovereign Lord of all. Through its manifestation all these names and attributes have been revealed, and by the suspension of its action they are all destroyed and perish.

It would be wholly untrue to maintain that this faculty is the same as the power of vision, inasmuch as the power of vision is derived from it and acteth in dependence upon it. It would, likewise, be idle to contend that this faculty can be identified with the sense of hearing, as the sense of hearing receiveth from the rational faculty the requisite energy for performing its functions.

This same relationship bindeth this faculty with whatsoever hath been the recipient of these names and attributes within the human temple. These diverse names and revealed attributes have been generated through the agency of this sign of God. Immeasurably exalted is this sign, in its essence and reality, above all such names and attributes. Nay, all else besides it will, when compared with its glory, fade into utter nothingness and become a thing forgotten.

Wert thou to ponder in thine heart, from now until the end that hath no end, and with all the concentrated intelligence and understanding which the greatest minds have attained in the past or will attain in the future, this divinely ordained and subtle Reality, this sign of the revelation of the All-Abiding, All-Glorious God, thou wilt fail to comprehend its mystery or to appraise its virtue. Having recognized thy powerlessness to attain to an adequate understanding of that Reality which abideth within thee, thou wilt readily admit the futility of such efforts as may be attempted by thee, or by any of the created things, to fathom the mystery of the Living God, the Day Star of unfading glory, the Ancient of everlasting days. This confession of helplessness which mature contemplation must eventually impel every mind to make is in itself the acme of human understanding, and marketh the culmination of man's development.

15

*S*pirit, mind, soul, and the powers of sight
and hearing are but one single reality which hath
manifold expressions owing to the diversity of its
instruments. As thou dost observe, man's power to
comprehend, move, speak, hear, and see all derive
from this sign of his Lord within him. It is single in
its essence, yet manifold through the diversity of its
instruments. This, verily, is a certain truth. For
example, if it directeth its attention to the means of
hearing, then hearing and its attributes become
manifest. Likewise, if it directeth itself to the means
of vision, a different effect and attribute appear.
Reflect upon this subject that thou mayest
comprehend the true meaning of what hath been
intended, find thyself independent of the sayings of
the people, and be of them that are well assured. In
like manner, when this sign of God turneth towards

the brain, the head, and such means, the powers of the mind and the soul are manifested.

16

*T*here are in the world of humanity three degrees; those of the body, the soul, and spirit.

The body is the physical or animal degree of man. From the bodily point of view man is a sharer of the animal kingdom. The bodies alike of men and animals are composed of elements held together by the law of attraction.

Like the animal, man possesses the faculties of the senses, is subject to heat, cold, hunger, thirst, etc.; unlike the animal, man has a rational soul, the human intelligence.

This intelligence of man is the intermediary between his body and his spirit.

When man allows the spirit, through his soul, to enlighten his understanding, then does he contain all Creation; because man, being the culmination of all that went before and thus superior to all previous evolutions, contains all the lower world within himself. Illumined by the spirit through the instrumentality of the soul, man's radiant intelligence makes him the crowning-point of Creation.

17

In man there are two natures; his spiritual or higher nature and his material or lower nature. In one he approaches God, in the other he lives for the world alone. Signs of both these natures are to be found in men. In his material aspect he expresses untruth, cruelty and injustice; all these are the outcome of his lower nature. The attributes of his Divine nature are shown forth in love, mercy, kindness, truth and justice, one and all being expressions of his higher nature. Every good habit, every noble quality belongs to man's spiritual nature, whereas all his imperfections and sinful actions are born of his material nature. If a man's Divine nature dominates his human nature, we have a saint.

Man has the power both to do good and to do evil; if his power for good predominates and his inclinations to do wrong are conquered, then man in truth may be called a saint. But if, on the contrary, he rejects the things of God and allows his evil passions to conquer him, then he is no better than a mere animal.

Saints are men who have freed themselves from the world of matter and who have overcome sin. They live in the world but are not of it, their thoughts being continually in the world of the spirit. Their lives are spent in holiness, and their deeds show forth love, justice and godliness. They are illumined from on high; they are as bright and shining lamps in the dark places of the earth. These are the saints of God. The apostles, who were the disciples of Jesus Christ, were just as other men are; they, like their fellows, were attracted by the things of the world, and each thought only of his own advantage. They knew little of justice, nor were the Divine perfections found in their midst. But when they followed Christ and believed in Him, their ignorance gave place to understanding, cruelty was changed to justice, falsehood to truth, darkness into light. They had been worldly, they became spiritual and divine. They had been children of darkness, they became sons of God, they became saints! Strive therefore to follow in their steps, leaving all worldly things behind, and striving to attain to the Spiritual Kingdom.

Pray to God that He may strengthen you in divine virtue, so that you may be as angels in the world, and beacons of light to disclose the mysteries of the Kingdom to those with understanding hearts.

18

*K*now that, although the human soul has existed on the earth for prolonged times and ages, yet it is phenomenal. As it is a divine sign, when once it has come into existence, it is eternal. The spirit of man has a beginning, but it has no end; it continues eternally. In the same way the species existing on this earth are phenomenal, for it is established that there was a time when these species did not exist on the surface of the earth. Moreover, the earth has not always existed, but the world of existence has always been, for the universe is not limited to this terrestrial globe. The meaning of this is that, although human souls are phenomenal, they are nevertheless immortal, everlasting and perpetual; for the world of things is the world of imperfection in comparison with that of man, and the world of man is the world of perfection in comparison with that of things.

When imperfections reach the station of perfection, they become eternal.

19

*S*pirit cannot be perceived by the material senses of the physical body, excepting as it is expressed in outward signs and works. The human body is visible, the soul is invisible. It is the soul nevertheless that directs a man's faculties, that governs his humanity.

The soul has two main faculties. (*a*) As outer circumstances are communicated to the soul by the eyes, ears, and brain of a man, so does the soul communicate its desires and purposes through the brain to the hands and tongue of the physical body, thereby expressing itself. The spirit in the soul is the very essence of life. (*b*) The second faculty of the soul expresses itself in the world of vision, where the soul inhabited by the spirit has its being, and functions without the help of the material bodily senses. There, in the realm of vision, the soul sees without the help of the physical eye, hears without the aid of the physical ear, and travels without dependence upon physical motion. It is, therefore, clear that the spirit in the soul of man can function through the physical body by using the organs of the ordinary senses, and that it is able also to live and act without their aid in the world of vision. This proves without a doubt the superiority of the soul of man over his body, the superiority of spirit over matter.

For example, look at this lamp: is not the light within it superior to the lamp which holds it? However beautiful the form of the lamp may be, if the light is not there its purpose is unfulfilled, it is without life—a dead thing. The lamp needs the light, but the light does not need the lamp.

The spirit does not need a body, but the body needs spirit, or it cannot live. The soul can live without a body, but the body without a soul dies.

If a man lose his sight, his hearing, his hand or his foot, should his soul still inhabit the body he lives, and is able to manifest divine virtues. On the other hand, without the spirit it would be impossible for a perfect body to exist.

20

God, in His Bounty, has given us a foretaste here, has given us certain proofs of the difference that exists between body, soul and spirit.

We see that cold, heat, suffering, etc, only concern the *body,* they do not touch the spirit.

How often do we see a man, poor, sick, miserably clad, and with no means of support, yet spiritually strong. Whatever his body has to suffer, his spirit is free and well! Again, how often do we see a rich man, physically strong and healthy, but with a soul sick unto death.

It is quite apparent to the seeing mind that a man's spirit is something very different from his physical body.

The spirit is changeless, indestructible. The progress and development of the soul, the joy and sorrow of the soul, are independent of the physical body.

If we are caused joy or pain by a friend, if a love prove true or false, it is the soul that is affected. If our dear ones are far from us—it is the soul that grieves, and the grief or trouble of the soul may react on the body.

Thus, when the spirit is fed with holy virtues, then is the body joyous; if the soul falls into sin, the body is in torment!

When we find truth, constancy, fidelity, and love, we are happy; but if we meet with lying, faithlessness, and deceit, we are miserable.

These are all things pertaining to the soul, and are not *bodily* ills. Thus, it is apparent that the soul, even as the body, has its own individuality. But if the body undergoes a change, the spirit need not be touched. When you break a glass on which the sun shines, the glass is broken, but the sun still shines! If a cage containing a bird is destroyed, the bird is unharmed! If a lamp is broken, the flame can still burn bright!

The same thing applies to the spirit of man. Though death destroy his body, it has no power over his spirit—this is eternal, everlasting, both birthless and deathless.

Spiritual Development

21

*K*now thou that all men have been created in the nature made by God, the Guardian, the Self-Subsisting. Unto each one hath been prescribed a pre-ordained measure, as decreed in God's mighty and guarded Tablets. All that which ye potentially possess can, however, be manifested only as a result of your own volition. Your own acts testify to this truth.

22

*K*now thou that every soul is fashioned after the nature of God, each being pure and holy at his birth. Afterwards, however, the individuals will vary according to what they acquire of virtues or vices in this world. Although all existent beings are in their very nature created in ranks or degrees, for capacities are various, nevertheless every individual is born holy and pure, and only thereafter may he become defiled.

23

*I*n the beginning of his human life man was embryonic in the world of the matrix. There he received capacity and endowment for the reality of human existence. The forces and powers necessary for this world were bestowed upon him in that limited condition. In this world he needed eyes; he received them potentially in the other. He needed ears; he obtained them there in readiness and preparation for his new existence. The powers requisite in this world were conferred upon him in the world of the matrix so that when he entered this realm of real existence he not only possessed all necessary functions and powers but found provision for his material sustenance awaiting him.

Therefore, in this world he must prepare himself for the life beyond. That which he needs in the world of the Kingdom must be obtained here. Just as he prepared himself in the world of the matrix by acquiring forces necessary in this sphere of existence, so, likewise, the indispensable forces of the divine existence must be potentially attained in this world.

24

*W*hat is he [man] in need of in the Kingdom which transcends the life and limitation of this mortal sphere? That world beyond is a world of sanctity and radiance; therefore, it is necessary that in this world he should acquire these divine attributes. In that world there is need of spirituality, faith, assurance, the knowledge and love of God. These he must attain in this world so that after his ascension from the earthly to the heavenly Kingdom he shall find all that is needful in that eternal life ready for him.

That divine world is manifestly a world of lights; therefore, man has need of illumination here. That is a world of love; the love of God is essential. It is a world of perfections; virtues, or perfections, must be acquired. That world is vivified by the breaths of the Holy Spirit; in this world we must seek them. That is the Kingdom of everlasting life; it must be attained during this vanishing existence.

By what means can man acquire these things? How shall he obtain these merciful gifts and powers? First, through the knowledge of God. Second, through the love of God. Third, through faith. Fourth, through philanthropic deeds. Fifth, through self-sacrifice. Sixth, through severance from this world. Seventh, through sanctity and holiness. Unless he acquires these forces and attains to these requirements, he will surely be deprived of the life that is eternal. But if he possesses the knowledge of God, becomes ignited through the fire of the love of God, witnesses the great and mighty signs of the Kingdom, becomes the cause of love among mankind and lives in the utmost state of sanctity and holiness, he shall surely attain to second birth, be baptized by the Holy Spirit and enjoy everlasting existence.

Is it not astonishing that although man has been created for the knowledge and love of God, for the virtues of the human world, for spirituality, heavenly illumination and eternal life, nevertheless, he continues ignorant and negligent of all this? Consider how he seeks knowledge of everything except knowledge of God. For instance, his utmost desire is to penetrate the mysteries of the lowest strata of the earth. Day by day he strives to know what can be found ten meters below the surface, what he can discover within the stone, what he can learn by archaeological research in the dust. He puts forth arduous labors to fathom terrestrial mysteries but is not at all concerned about knowing the mysteries of the Kingdom, traversing the illimitable fields of the eternal world, becoming informed of the divine realities, discovering the secrets of God, attaining the knowledge of God, witnessing the splendors of the Sun of Truth and realizing the glories of everlasting life. He is unmindful and thoughtless of these. How much he is attracted to the mysteries of matter, and how completely unaware he is of the mysteries of Divinity! Nay, he is utterly negligent and oblivious of the secrets of Divinity. How great his ignorance! How conducive to his degradation! It is as if a kind and loving father had provided a library of wonderful books for his son in order that he might be informed of the mysteries of creation, at the same time surrounding him with every means of comfort and enjoyment, but the son amuses himself with pebbles and playthings, neglectful of all his father's gifts and provision. How ignorant and heedless is man! The Father has willed for him eternal glory, and he is content with blindness and deprivation. The Father has built for him a royal palace, but he is playing with the dust; prepared for him garments of silk, but he prefers to remain unclothed; provided for him delicious foods and fruits, while he seeks sustenance in the grasses of the field.

25

*M*an must sever himself from the influences of the world of matter, from the world of nature and its laws; for the material world is the world of corruption and death. It is the world of evil and darkness, of animalism and ferocity, bloodthirstiness, ambition and avarice, of self-worship, egotism and passion; it is the world of nature. Man must strip himself of all these imperfections, must sacrifice these tendencies which are peculiar to the outer and material world of existence.

On the other hand, man must acquire heavenly qualities and attain divine attributes. He must become the image and likeness of God. He must seek the bounty of the eternal, become the manifestor of the love of God, the light of guidance, the tree of life and the depository of the bounties of

God. That is to say, man must sacrifice the qualities and attributes of the world of nature for the qualities and attributes of the world of God. For instance, consider the substance we call iron. Observe its qualities; it is solid, black, cold. These are the characteristics of iron. When the same iron absorbs heat from the fire, it sacrifices its attribute of solidity for the attribute of fluidity. It sacrifices its attribute of darkness for the attribute of light, which is a quality of the fire. It sacrifices its attribute of coldness to the quality of heat which the fire possesses so that in the iron there remains no solidity, darkness or cold. It becomes illumined and transformed, having sacrificed its qualities to the qualities and attributes of the fire.

Likewise, man, when separated and severed from the attributes of the world of nature, sacrifices the qualities and exigencies of that mortal realm and manifests the perfections of the Kingdom, just as the qualities of the iron disappeared and the qualities of the fire appeared in their place.

Every man trained through the teachings of God and illumined by the light of His guidance, who becomes a believer in God and His signs and is enkindled with the fire of the love of God, sacrifices the imperfections of nature for the sake of divine perfections. Consequently, every perfect person, every illumined, heavenly individual stands in the station of sacrifice. . . . May the divine light become manifest upon your faces, the fragrances of holiness refresh your nostrils and the breath of the Holy Spirit quicken you with eternal life.

26

The retina of outer vision, though sensitive and delicate, may, nevertheless, be a hindrance to the inner eye which alone can perceive. The bestowals of God which are manifest in all phenomenal life are sometimes hidden by intervening veils of mental and mortal vision which render man spiritually blind and incapable, but when those scales are removed and the veils rent asunder, then the great signs of God will become visible, and he will witness the eternal light filling the world. The bestowals of God are all and always manifest. The promises of heaven are ever present. The favors of God are all-surrounding, but should the conscious eye of the soul of man remain veiled and darkened, he will be led to deny these universal signs and remain deprived of these manifestations of divine bounty. Therefore, we must endeavor with heart and soul in order that the veil covering the eye of inner vision may be removed, that we may behold the manifestations of the signs of God, discern His mysterious graces and realize that material blessings as compared with spiritual bounties are as nothing. The spiritual blessings of God are greatest. When we were in the mineral kingdom, although we were endowed with certain gifts and powers, they were not to be compared with the blessings of the human kingdom. In the matrix of the mother we were the recipients of endowments and blessings of God, yet these were as nothing compared to the powers and graces bestowed upon us after birth into this human world. Likewise, if we are born from the matrix of this physical and phenomenal environment into the freedom and loftiness of the spiritual life and vision, we shall consider this mortal existence and its blessings as worthless by comparison.

In the spiritual world the divine bestowals are infinite, for in that realm there is neither separation nor disintegration, which characterize the world of material existence. Spiritual existence is absolute immortality, completeness and unchangeable being. Therefore, we must thank God that He has created for us both material blessings and spiritual bestowals. He has given us material gifts and spiritual graces, outer sight to view the lights of the sun and inner

vision by which we may perceive the glory of God.
He has designed the outer ear to enjoy the melodies
of sound and the inner hearing wherewith we may
hear the voice of our Creator. We must strive with
energies of heart, soul and mind to develop and
manifest the perfections and virtues latent within the
realities of the phenomenal world, for the human
reality may be compared to a seed. If we sow the
seed, a mighty tree appears from it. The virtues of the
seed are revealed in the tree; it puts forth branches,
leaves, blossoms, and produces fruits. All these virtues
were hidden and potential in the seed. Through the
blessing and bounty of cultivation these virtues
became apparent. Similarly, the merciful God, our
Creator, has deposited within human realities certain
latent and potential virtues. Through education and
culture these virtues deposited by the loving God
will become apparent in the human reality, even as
the unfoldment of the tree from within the
germinating seed.

27

*T*he greatest attainment in the world of
humanity is nearness to God. Every lasting glory,
honor, grace and beauty which comes to man comes
through nearness to God. All the Prophets and
apostles longed and prayed for nearness to the
Creator. How many nights they passed in sleepless
yearning for this station; how many days they
devoted to supplication for this attainment, seeking
ever to draw nigh unto Him! But nearness to God is
not an easy accomplishment. During the time Jesus
Christ was upon the earth mankind sought nearness
to God, but in that day no one attained it save a very
few—His disciples. Those blessed souls were
confirmed with divine nearness through the love of
God. Divine nearness is dependent upon attainment
to the knowledge of God, upon severance from all
else save God. It is contingent upon self-sacrifice and

to be found only through forfeiting wealth and worldly possessions. It is made possible through the baptism of water and fire revealed in the Gospels. Water symbolizes the water of life, which is knowledge, and fire is the fire of the love of God; therefore, man must be baptized with the water of life, the Holy Spirit and the fire of the love of the Kingdom. Until he attains these three degrees, nearness to God is not possible. . . . And be it known that this nearness is not dependent upon time or place. Nearness to God is dependent upon purity of the heart and exhilaration of the spirit through the glad tidings of the Kingdom. Consider how a pure, well-polished mirror fully reflects the effulgence of the sun, no matter how distant the sun may be. As soon as the mirror is cleaned and purified, the sun will manifest itself. The more pure and sanctified the heart of man becomes, the nearer it draws to God, and the light of the Sun of Reality is revealed within it. This light sets hearts aglow with the fire of the love of God, opens in them the doors of knowledge and unseals the divine mysteries so that spiritual discoveries are made possible. All the Prophets have drawn near to God through severance. We must emulate those Holy Souls and renounce our own wishes and desires. We must purify ourselves from the mire and soil of earthly contact until our hearts become as mirrors in clearness and the light of the most great guidance reveals itself in them.

28

The soul does not evolve from degree to degree as a law—it only evolves nearer to God, by the Mercy and Bounty of God.

29

*N*earness to God is possible through devotion to Him, through entrance into the Kingdom and service to humanity; it is attained by unity with mankind and through loving-kindness to all; it is dependent upon investigation of truth, acquisition of praiseworthy virtues, service in the cause of universal peace and personal sanctification. In a word, nearness to God necessitates sacrifice of self, severance and the giving up of all to Him. Nearness is likeness.

Behold how the sun shines upon all creation, but only surfaces that are pure and polished can reflect its glory and light. The darkened soul has no portion of the revelation of the glorious effulgence of reality; and the soil of self, unable to take advantage of that light, does not produce growth. The eyes of the blind cannot behold the rays of the sun; only pure eyes with sound and perfect sight can receive them. Green and living trees can absorb the bounty of the sun; dead roots and withered branches are destroyed by it. Therefore, man must seek capacity and develop readiness. As long as he lacks susceptibility to divine influences, he is incapable of reflecting the light and assimilating its benefits. Sterile soil will produce nothing, even if the cloud of mercy pours rain upon it a thousand years. We must make the soil of our hearts receptive and fertile by tilling in order that the rain of divine mercy may refresh them and bring forth roses and hyacinths of heavenly planting. We must have perceiving eyes in order to see the light of the sun. We must cleanse the nostril in order to scent the fragrances of the divine rose garden. We must render the ears attentive in order to hear the summons of the supreme Kingdom. No matter how beautiful the melody, the ear that is deaf cannot hear it, cannot receive the call of the Supreme Concourse. The nostril that is clogged with dust cannot inhale the fragrant odors of the blossoms. Therefore, we must ever strive for capacity and seek readiness. As long as we lack susceptibility, the beauties and bounties of God cannot penetrate. Christ spoke a parable in which He said His words were like the seeds of the sower; some fall upon stony ground, some upon sterile soil, some are choked by thorns and thistles, but some fall upon the ready, receptive and fertile ground of human hearts. When seeds are cast upon sterile soil, no growth follows. Those cast upon stony ground will grow a short time, but lacking deep roots will wither away. Thorns and thistles destroy others completely, but the seed cast in good ground brings forth harvest and fruitage.

Consider how the parable makes attainment dependent upon capacity. Unless capacity is developed, the summons of the Kingdom cannot reach the ear, the light of the Sun of Truth will not be observed, and the fragrances of the rose garden of inner significance will be lost. Let us endeavor to attain capacity, susceptibility and worthiness that we may hear the call of the glad tidings of the Kingdom, become revivified by the breaths of the Holy Spirit, hoist the standard of the oneness of humanity, establish human brotherhood, and under the protection of divine grace attain the everlasting and eternal life.

30

*A*bsolute repose does not exist in nature. All things either make progress or lose ground. Everything moves forward or backward, nothing is without motion. From his birth, a man progresses physically until he reaches maturity, then, having arrived at the prime of his life, he begins to decline, the strength and powers of his body decrease, and he gradually arrives at the hour of death. Likewise a plant progresses from the seed to maturity, then its life begins to lessen until it fades and dies. A bird soars to a certain height and having reached the highest possible point in its flight, begins its descent to earth.

Thus it is evident that movement is essential to all existence. All material things progress to a certain point, then begin to decline. This is the law which governs the whole physical creation.

Now let us consider the soul. We have seen that movement is essential to existence; nothing that has life is without motion. All creation, whether of the mineral, vegetable or animal kingdom, is compelled to obey the law of motion; it must either ascend or descend. But with the human soul, there is no decline. Its only movement is towards perfection; growth and progress alone constitute the motion of the soul.

Divine perfection is infinite, therefore the progress of the soul is also infinite. From the very birth of a human being the soul progresses, the intellect grows and knowledge increases. When the body dies the soul lives on. All the differing degrees of created physical beings are limited, but the soul is limitless!

In all religions the belief exists that the soul survives the death of the body. Intercessions are sent up for the beloved dead, prayers are said for their progress and for the forgiveness of their sins. If the soul perished with the body all this would have no meaning. Further, if it were not possible for the soul to advance towards perfection after it had been released from the body, of what avail are all these loving prayers, of devotion?

We read in the sacred writings that "all good works are found again."* Now, if the soul did not survive, this also would mean nothing!

The very fact that our spiritual instinct, surely never given in vain, prompts us to pray for the welfare of those, our loved ones, who have passed out of the material world: does it not bear witness to the continuance of their existence?

In the world of spirit there is no retrogression. The world of mortality is a world of contradictions, of opposites; motion being compulsory everything must either go forward or retreat. In the realm of spirit there is no retreat possible, all movement is bound to be towards a perfect state. "Progress" is the expression of spirit in the world of matter. The intelligence of man, his reasoning powers, his knowledge, his scientific achievements, all these being manifestations of the spirit, partake of the inevitable law of spiritual progress and are, therefore, of necessity, immortal.

My hope for you is that you will progress in the world of spirit, as well as in the world of matter; that your intelligence will develop, your knowledge will augment, and your understanding be widened.

---

* That is, all good actions bring their own reward.

You must ever press forward, never standing still; avoid stagnation, the first step to a backward movement, to decay.

31

*W*hen man does not open his mind and heart to the blessing of the spirit, but turns his soul towards the material side, towards the bodily part of his nature, then is he fallen from his high place and he becomes inferior to the inhabitants of the lower animal kingdom. In this case the man is in a sorry plight! For if the spiritual qualities of the soul, open to the breath of the Divine Spirit, are never used, they become atrophied, enfeebled, and at last incapable; whilst the soul's material qualities alone being exercised, they become terribly powerful—and the unhappy, misguided man, becomes more savage, more unjust, more vile, more cruel, more malevolent than the lower animals themselves. All his aspirations and desires being strengthened by the lower side of the soul's nature, he becomes more and more brutal, until his whole being is in no way superior to that of

the beasts that perish. Men such as this plan to work
evil, to hurt and to destroy; they are entirely without
the spirit of Divine compassion, for the celestial
quality of the soul has been dominated by that of the
material. If, on the contrary, the spiritual nature of
the soul has been so strengthened that it holds the
material side in subjection, then does the man
approach the Divine; his humanity becomes so
glorified that the virtues of the Celestial Assembly
are manifested in him; he radiates the Mercy of God,
he stimulates the spiritual progress of mankind, for
he becomes a lamp to show light on their path.

You perceive how the soul is the intermediary
between the body and the spirit. In like manner is
this tree* the intermediary between the seed and the
fruit. When the fruit of the tree appears and becomes
ripe, then we know that the tree is perfect; if the tree
bore no fruit it would be merely a useless growth,
serving no purpose!

When a soul has in it the life of the spirit, then
does it bring forth good fruit and become a Divine
tree. I wish you to try to understand this example. I
hope that the unspeakable goodness of God will so
strengthen you that the celestial quality of your soul,
which relates it to the spirit, will for ever dominate

---

* A small orange-tree on the table nearby.

the material side, so entirely ruling the senses that your soul will approach the perfections of the Heavenly Kingdom. May your faces, being steadfastly set towards the Divine Light, become so luminous that all your thoughts, words and actions will shine with the Spiritual Radiance dominating your souls, so that in the gatherings of the world you will show perfection in your life.

Some men's lives are solely occupied with the things of this world; their minds are so circumscribed by exterior manners and traditional interests that they are blind to any other realm of existence, to the spiritual significance of all things! They think and dream of earthly fame, of material progress. Sensuous delights and comfortable surroundings bound their horizon, their highest ambitions centre in successes of worldly conditions and circumstances! They curb not their lower propensities; they eat, drink, and sleep! Like the animal, they have no thought beyond their own physical well-being. It is true that these necessities must be despatched. Life is a load which must be carried on while we are on earth, but the cares of the lower things of life should not be allowed to monopolize all the thoughts and aspirations of a human being. The heart's ambitions should ascend to a more glorious goal, mental activity should rise to higher levels! Men should hold in their souls the vision of celestial perfection, and there prepare a dwelling-place for the inexhaustible bounty of the Divine Spirit.

Let your ambition be the achievement on earth of a Heavenly civilization! I ask for you the supreme blessing, that you may be so filled with the vitality of the Heavenly Spirit that you may be the cause of life to the world.

32

*N*o matter how much the physical body of man is trained and developed, there will be no real progression in the human station unless the mind correspondingly advances. No matter how much man may acquire material virtues, he will not be able to realize and express the highest possibilities of life without spiritual graces. God has created all earthly things under a law of progression in material degrees, but He has created man and endowed him with powers of advancement toward spiritual and transcendental kingdoms. He has not created material phenomena after His own image and likeness, but He has created man after that image and with potential power to attain that likeness. He has distinguished man above all other created things. All created things except man are captives of nature and the sense world, but in man there has been created an ideal power by which he may perceive intellectual or spiritual realities. He has brought forth everything necessary for the life of this world, but man is a creation intended for the reflection of divine virtues. Consider that the highest type of creation below man is the animal, which is superior to all degrees of life except man. Manifestly, the animal has been created for the life of this world. Its highest virtue is to express excellence in the material plane of existence. The animal is perfect when its body is healthy and its physical senses are whole. When it is characterized by the attributes of physical health, when its physical forces are in working order, when food and surrounding conditions minister to its needs, it has attained the ultimate perfection of its kingdom. But man does not depend upon these things for his virtues. No matter how perfect his health and physical powers, if that is all, he has not yet risen above the degree of a perfect animal. Beyond and above this, God has opened the doors of ideal virtues and attainments before the face of man. He has created in his being the mysteries of the divine Kingdom. He has bestowed upon him the power of intellect so that through the attribute of reason, when fortified by the Holy Spirit, he may penetrate and discover ideal realities and become informed of the mysteries of the world of significances. As this power to penetrate the ideal knowledges is superhuman, supernatural, man becomes the collective center of spiritual as well as material forces so that the divine spirit may manifest itself in his being, the effulgences of the Kingdom shine within the sanctuary of his heart, the signs of the attributes and perfections of God reveal themselves in a newness of life, the everlasting glory and eternal existence be attained, the knowledge of God illumine, and the mysteries of the realm of might be unsealed.

Man is like unto this lamp, but the effulgences of the Kingdom are like the rays of the lamp. Man is like unto the glass, but spiritual splendors are like unto the light within the glass. No matter how translucent the glass may be, as long as there is no light within, it remains dark. Likewise, man, no matter how much he advances in material accomplishments, will remain like the glass without light if he is deprived of the spiritual virtues. Material virtues are like unto a perfect body, but this body is in need of the spirit. No matter how handsome and perfect the body may be, if it is deprived of the spirit and its animus, it is dead. But when that same body is affiliated with the spirit and

expressing life, perfection and virtue become realized
in it. Deprived of the Holy Spirit and its bounties,
man is spiritually dead.

Children, for instance, no matter how good and
pure, no matter how healthy their bodies, are,
nevertheless, considered imperfect because the power
of intellect is not fully manifest in them. When the
intellectual power fully displays its influences and
they attain to the age of maturity, they are considered
as perfect. Likewise, man, no matter how much he
may advance in worldly affairs and make progress in
material civilization, is imperfect unless he is
quickened by the bounties of the Holy Spirit; for it is
evident that until he receives that divine impetus he
is ignorant and deprived. For this reason Jesus Christ
said, "Except a man be born of water and of the
Spirit, he cannot enter into the kingdom of God." By
this Christ meant that unless man is released from
the material world, freed from the captivity of
materialism and receiving a portion of the bounties
of the spiritual world, he shall be deprived of the
bestowals and favors of the Kingdom of God, and the
utmost we can say of him is that he is a perfect
animal. No one can rightly call him a man. In
another place He said, "That which is born of the
flesh is flesh; and that which is born of the Spirit is
spirit." The meaning of this is that if man is a captive

of nature, he is like unto an animal because he is only a body physically born—that is, he belongs to the world of matter and remains subject to the law and control of nature. But if he is baptized with the Holy Spirit, if he is freed from the bondage of nature, released from animalistic tendencies and advanced in the human realm, he is fitted to enter into the divine Kingdom. The world of the Kingdom is the realm of divine bestowals and the bounties of God. It is attainment of the highest virtues of humanity; it is nearness to God; it is capacity to receive the bounties of the ancient Lord. When man advances to this station, he attains the second birth. Before his first or physical birth man was in the world of the matrix. He had no knowledge of this world; his eyes could not see; his ears could not hear. When he was born from the world of the matrix, he beheld another world. The sun was shining with its splendors, the moon radiant in the heavens, the stars twinkling in the expansive firmament, the seas surging, trees verdant and green, all kinds of creatures enjoying life here, infinite bounties prepared for him. In the world of the matrix none of these things existed. In that world he had no knowledge of this vast range of existence; nay, rather, he would have denied the reality of this world. But after his birth he began to open his eyes and behold the wonders of this illimitable universe. Similarly, as long as man is in the matrix of the human world, as long as he is the captive of nature, he is out of touch and without knowledge of the universe of the Kingdom. If he attains rebirth while in the world of nature, he will become informed of the divine world. He will observe that another and a higher world exists. Wonderful bounties descend; eternal life awaits; everlasting glory surrounds him. All the signs of reality and greatness are there. He will see the lights of God. All these experiences will be his when he is born out of the world of nature into the divine world. Therefore, for the perfect man there are two kinds of birth: the first, physical birth, is from the matrix of the mother; the second, or spiritual birth, is from the world of nature. In both he is without knowledge of the new world of existence he is entering. Therefore, rebirth means his release from the captivity of nature, freedom from attachment to this mortal and material life. This is the second, or spiritual, birth of which Jesus Christ spoke in the Gospels.

33

*Y*ou have asked why it was necessary for the soul that was from God to make this journey back to God?

Would you like to understand the reality of this question just as I teach it, or do you wish to hear it as the world teaches it? For if I should answer you according to the latter way, this would be but imitation and would not make the subject clear.

The reality underlying this question is that the evil spirit, Satan or whatever is interpreted as evil, refers to the lower nature in man. This baser nature is symbolized in various ways. In man there are two expressions: One is the expression of nature; the other, the expression of the spiritual realm. The world of nature is defective. Look at it clearly, casting aside all superstition and imagination. If you should leave a man uneducated and barbarous in the wilds of Africa, would there be any doubt about his remaining ignorant? God has never created an evil spirit; all such ideas and nomenclature are symbols expressing the mere human or earthly nature of man. It is an essential condition of the soil of earth that thorns, weeds and fruitless trees may grow from it. Relatively speaking, this is evil; it is simply the lower state and baser product of nature.

It is evident, therefore, that man is in need of divine education and inspiration, that the spirit and bounties of God are essential to his development. That is to say, the teachings of Christ and the Prophets are necessary for his education and guidance. Why? Because They are the divine Gardeners Who till the earth of human hearts and minds. They educate man, uproot the weeds, burn the thorns and remodel the waste places into gardens and orchards where fruitful trees grow. The wisdom and purpose of Their training is that man must pass from degree to degree of progressive unfoldment until perfection is attained. For instance, if a man should live his entire life in one city, he cannot gain a knowledge of the whole world. To become perfectly informed he must visit other cities, see the mountains and valleys, cross the rivers and traverse the plains. In other words, without progressive and universal education perfection will not be attained.

Man must walk in many paths and be subjected to various processes in his evolution upward. Physically he is not born in full stature but passes through consecutive stages of fetus, infant, childhood, youth, maturity and old age. Suppose he had the power to remain young throughout his life. He then would not understand the meaning of old age and could not believe it existed. If he could not realize the condition of old age, he would not know that he was young. He would not know the difference between young and old without experiencing the old. Unless you have passed through the state of infancy, how would you know this was an infant beside you? If there were no wrong, how would you recognize the right? If it were not for sin, how would you appreciate virtue? If evil deeds were unknown, how could you commend good actions? If sickness did not exist, how would you understand health? Evil is nonexistent; it is the absence of good. Sickness is the loss of health; poverty, the lack of riches. When wealth disappears, you are poor; you look within the treasure box but find nothing there. Without knowledge there is ignorance; therefore, ignorance is simply the lack of knowledge. Death is the absence of life. Therefore, on the one hand, we have existence; on the other, nonexistence, negation or absence of existence.

Briefly, the journey of the soul is necessary. The pathway of life is the road which leads to divine knowledge and attainment. Without training and guidance the soul could never progress beyond the conditions of its lower nature, which is ignorant and defective.

34

*I*t behooves man to abandon thoughts of nonexistence and death, which are absolutely imaginary, and see himself ever-living, everlasting in the divine purpose of his creation. He must turn away from ideas which degrade the human soul so that day by day and hour by hour he may advance upward and higher to spiritual perception of the continuity of the human reality. If he dwells upon the thought of nonexistence, he will become utterly incompetent; with weakened willpower his ambition for progress will be lessened and the acquisition of human virtues will cease.

Therefore, you must thank God that He has bestowed upon you the blessing of life and existence in the human kingdom. Strive diligently to acquire virtues befitting your degree and station. Be as lights of the world which cannot be hid and which have no setting in horizons of darkness. Ascend to the zenith of an existence which is never beclouded by the fears and forebodings of nonexistence.

35

To consider that after the death of the body the spirit perishes is like imagining that a bird in a cage will be destroyed if the cage is broken, though the bird has nothing to fear from the destruction of the cage. Our body is like the cage, and the spirit is like the bird. We see that without the cage this bird flies in the world of sleep; therefore, if the cage becomes broken, the bird will continue and exist. Its feelings will be even more powerful, its perceptions greater, and its happiness increased. In truth, from hell it reaches a paradise of delights because for the thankful birds there is no paradise greater than freedom from the cage.

Immortality and
Life Hereafter

36

Through his ignorance man fears death, but the death he shrinks from is imaginary and absolutely unreal; it is only human imagination.

37

These human conditions may be likened to the matrix of the mother from which a child is to be born into the spacious outer world. At first the infant finds it very difficult to reconcile itself to its new existence. It cries as if not wishing to be separated from its narrow abode and imagining that life is restricted to that limited space. It is reluctant to leave its home, but nature forces it into this world. Having come into its new conditions, it finds that it has passed from darkness into a sphere of radiance; from gloomy and restricted surroundings it has been transferred to a spacious and delightful environment. Its nourishment was the blood of the mother; now it finds delicious food to enjoy. Its new life is filled with brightness and beauty; it looks with wonder and delight upon the mountains, meadows and fields of green, the rivers and fountains, the wonderful stars; it breathes the life-quickening atmosphere; and then it praises God for its release from the confinement of its former condition and attainment to the freedom of a new realm. This analogy expresses the relation of the temporal world to the life hereafter—the transition of the soul of man from darkness and uncertainty to the light and reality of the eternal Kingdom. At first it is very difficult to welcome death, but after attaining its new condition the soul is grateful, for it has been released from the bondage of the limited to enjoy the liberties of the unlimited. It has been freed from a world of sorrow, grief and trials to live in a world of unending bliss and joy. The phenomenal and physical have been abandoned in order that it may attain the opportunities of the ideal and spiritual.

38

A friend asked: "How should one look forward to death?"

'Abdu'l-Bahá answered: "How does one look forward to the goal of any journey? With hope and with expectation. It is even so with the end of this earthly journey. In the next world, man will find himself freed from many of the disabilities under which he now suffers. Those who have passed on through death, have a sphere of their own. It is not removed from ours; their work, the work of the Kingdom, is ours; but it is sanctified from what we call 'time and place.' Time with us is measured by the sun. When there is no more sunrise, and no more sunset, that kind of time does not exist for man. Those who have ascended have different attributes from those who are still on earth, yet there is no real separation.

"In prayer there is a mingling of station, a mingling of condition. Pray for them as they pray for you! When you do not know it, and are in a receptive attitude, they are able to make suggestions to you, if you are in difficulty. This sometimes happens in sleep. But there is no phenomenal intercourse! That which seems like phenomenal intercourse has another explanation."

39

Thou hast ... asked Me concerning the state of the soul after its separation from the body. Know thou, of a truth, that if the soul of man hath walked in the ways of God, it will, assuredly, return and be gathered to the glory of the Beloved. By the righteousness of God! It shall attain a station such as no pen can depict, or tongue describe. The soul that hath remained faithful to the Cause of God, and stood unwaveringly firm in His Path shall, after his ascension, be possessed of such power that all the worlds which the Almighty hath created can benefit through him. Such a soul provideth, at the bidding of the Ideal King and Divine Educator, the pure leaven that leaveneth the world of being, and furnisheth the power through which the arts and wonders of the world are made manifest. Consider how meal needeth leaven to be leavened with. Those souls that are the symbols of detachment are the leaven of the world. Meditate on this, and be of the thankful.

40

*K*now thou of a truth that the soul, after its separation from the body, will continue to progress until it attaineth the presence of God, in a state and condition which neither the revolution of ages and centuries, nor the changes and chances of this world, can alter. It will endure as long as the Kingdom of God, His sovereignty, His dominion and power will endure. It will manifest the signs of God and His attributes, and will reveal His loving-kindness and bounty. The movement of My Pen is stilled when it attempteth to befittingly describe the loftiness and glory of so exalted a station. The honor with which the Hand of Mercy will invest the soul is such as no tongue can adequately reveal, nor any other earthly agency describe. Blessed is the soul which, at the hour of its separation from the body, is sanctified from the vain imaginings of the peoples of the world. Such a soul liveth and moveth in accordance with the Will of its Creator, and entereth the all-highest Paradise. The Maids of Heaven, inmates of the loftiest mansions, will circle around it, and the Prophets of God and His chosen ones will seek its companionship. With them that soul will freely converse, and will recount unto them that which it hath been made to endure in the path of God, the Lord of all worlds. If any man be told that which hath been ordained for such a soul in the worlds of God, the Lord of the throne on high and of earth below, his whole being will instantly blaze out in his great longing to attain that most exalted, that sanctified and resplendent station. . . .

41

*K*now ye that the world and its vanities and its embellishments shall pass away. Nothing will endure except God's Kingdom which pertaineth to none but Him, the Sovereign Lord of all, the Help in Peril, the All-Glorious, the Almighty. The days of your life shall roll away, and all the things with which ye are occupied and of which ye boast yourselves shall perish, and ye shall, most certainly, be summoned by a company of His angels to appear at the spot where the limbs of the entire creation shall be made to tremble, and the flesh of every oppressor to creep. Ye shall be asked of the things your hands have wrought in this, your vain life, and shall be repaid for your doings. This is the day that shall inevitably come upon you, the hour that none can put back. To this the Tongue of Him that speaketh the truth and is the Knower of all things hath testified.

42

O SON OF BEING!

Bring thyself to account each day ere thou art
summoned to a reckoning; for death, unheralded,
shall come upon thee and thou shalt be called to give
account for thy deeds.

43

The nature of the soul after death can never be described, nor is it meet and permissible to reveal its whole character to the eyes of men.... The world beyond is as different from this world as this world is different from that of the child while still in the womb of its mother. When the soul attaineth the Presence of God, it will assume the form that best befitteth its immortality and is worthy of its celestial habitation. Such an existence is a contingent and not an absolute existence, inasmuch as the former is preceded by a cause, whilst the latter is independent thereof. Absolute existence is strictly confined to God, exalted be His glory. Well is it with them that apprehend this truth. Wert thou to ponder in thine heart the behavior of the Prophets of God thou wouldst assuredly and readily testify that there must needs be other worlds besides this world. The majority of the truly wise and learned have, throughout the ages, as it hath been recorded by the Pen of Glory in the Tablet of Wisdom, borne witness to the truth of that which the holy Writ of God hath revealed. Even the materialists have testified in their writings to the wisdom of these divinely-appointed Messengers, and have regarded the references made by the Prophets to Paradise, to hell fire, to future reward and punishment, to have been actuated by a desire to educate and uplift the souls of men. Consider, therefore, how the generality of mankind, whatever their beliefs or theories, have recognized the excellence, and admitted the superiority, of these Prophets of God. These Gems of Detachment are acclaimed by some as the embodiments of wisdom, while others believe them to be the mouthpiece of God Himself. How could such Souls have consented to surrender themselves unto their enemies if they believed all the worlds of God to have been reduced to this earthly life? Would they have willingly suffered such afflictions and torments as no man hath ever experienced or witnessed?

44

*I*t is clear and evident that all men shall, after their physical death, estimate the worth of their deeds, and realize all that their hands have wrought. I swear by the Day Star that shineth above the horizon of Divine power! They that are the followers of the one true God shall, the moment they depart out of this life, experience such joy and gladness as would be impossible to describe, while they that live in error shall be seized with such fear and trembling, and shall be filled with such consternation, as nothing can exceed. Well is it with him that hath quaffed the choice and incorruptible wine of faith through the gracious favor and the manifold bounties of Him Who is the Lord of all Faiths. . . .

45

Thou hast asked Me whether man, as apart from the Prophets of God and His chosen ones, will retain, after his physical death, the self-same individuality, personality, consciousness, and understanding that characterize his life in this world. If this should be the case, how is it, thou hast observed, that whereas such slight injuries to his mental faculties as fainting and severe illness deprive him of his understanding and consciousness, his death, which must involve the decomposition of his body and the dissolution of its elements, is powerless to destroy that understanding and extinguish that consciousness? How can any one imagine that man's consciousness and personality will be maintained, when the very instruments necessary to their existence and function will have completely disintegrated?

Know thou that the soul of man is exalted above, and is independent of all infirmities of body or mind. That a sick person showeth signs of weakness is due to the hindrances that interpose themselves between his soul and his body, for the soul itself remaineth unaffected by any bodily ailments. Consider the light of the lamp. Though an external object may interfere with its radiance, the light itself continueth to shine with undiminished power. In like manner, every malady afflicting the body of man is an impediment that preventeth the soul from manifesting its inherent might and power. When it leaveth the body, however, it will evince such ascendancy, and reveal such influence as no force on earth can equal. Every pure, every refined and sanctified soul will be endowed with tremendous power, and shall rejoice with exceeding gladness.

Consider the lamp which is hidden under a bushel. Though its light be shining, yet its radiance is concealed from men. Likewise, consider the sun which hath been obscured by the clouds. Observe how its splendor appeareth to have diminished, when in reality the source of that light hath remained unchanged. The soul of man should be likened unto this sun, and all things on earth should be regarded as his body. So long as no external impediment interveneth between them, the body will, in its entirety, continue to reflect the light of the soul, and to be sustained by its power. As soon as, however, a veil interposeth itself between them, the brightness of that light seemeth to lessen.

Consider again the sun when it is completely hidden behind the clouds. Though the earth is still illumined with its light, yet the measure of light which it receiveth is considerably reduced. Not until the clouds have dispersed, can the sun shine again in the plenitude of its glory. Neither the presence of the cloud nor its absence can, in any way, affect the inherent splendor of the sun. The soul of man is the sun by which his body is illumined, and from which it draweth its sustenance, and should be so regarded.

Consider, moreover, how the fruit, ere it is formed, lieth potentially within the tree. Were the tree to be cut into pieces, no sign nor any part of the fruit, however small, could be detected. When it appeareth, however, it manifesteth itself, as thou hast observed, in its wondrous beauty and glorious perfection. Certain fruits, indeed, attain their fullest development only after being severed from the tree.

46

As to the soul of man after death, it remains in the degree of purity to which it has evolved during life in the physical body, and after it is freed from the body it remains plunged in the ocean of God's Mercy.

From the moment the soul leaves the body and arrives in the Heavenly World, its evolution is spiritual, and that evolution is: *The approaching unto God*.

In the physical creation, evolution is from one degree of perfection to another. The mineral passes with its mineral perfections to the vegetable; the vegetable, with its perfections, passes to the animal world, and so on to that of humanity. This world is full of seeming contradictions; in each of these kingdoms (mineral, vegetable and animal) life exists in its degree; though when compared to the life in a man, the earth appears to be dead, yet she, too, lives and has a life of her own. In this world things live and die, and live again in other forms of life, but in the world of the spirit it is quite otherwise.

The soul does not evolve from degree to degree as a law—it only evolves nearer to God, by the Mercy and Bounty of God.

47

The whole physical creation is perishable. These material bodies are composed of atoms; when these atoms begin to separate decomposition sets in, then comes what we call death. This composition of atoms, which constitutes the body or mortal element of any created being, is temporary. When the power of attraction, which holds these atoms together, is withdrawn, the body, as such, ceases to exist.

With the soul it is different. The soul is not a combination of elements, it is not composed of many atoms, it is of one indivisible substance and therefore eternal. It is entirely out of the order of the physical creation; it is immortal!

Scientific philosophy has demonstrated that a *simple* element ("simple" meaning "not composed") is indestructible, eternal. The soul, not being a composition of elements, is, in character, as a simple element, and therefore cannot cease to exist.

The soul, being of that one indivisible substance, can suffer neither disintegration nor destruction, therefore there is no reason for its coming to an end. All things living show signs of their existence, and it follows that these signs could not of themselves exist if that which they express or to which they testify had no being. A thing which does not exist, can, of course, give no sign of its existence. The manifold signs of the existence of the spirit are for ever before us.

The traces of the Spirit of Jesus Christ, the influence of His Divine Teaching, is present with us today, and is everlasting.

A non-existent thing, it is agreed, cannot be seen by signs. In order to write a man must exist—one who does not exist cannot write. Writing is, in itself, a sign of the writer's soul and intelligence. The Sacred Writings (with ever the same Teaching) prove the continuity of the spirit.

Consider the aim of creation: is it possible that all is created to evolve and develop through countless ages with this small goal in view—a few years of a man's life on earth? Is it not unthinkable that this should be the final aim of existence?

The mineral evolves till it is absorbed in the life of the plant, the plant progresses till finally it loses its life in that of the animal; the animal, in its turn, forming part of the food of man, is absorbed into human life.

Thus, man is shown to be the sum of all creation, the superior of all created beings, the goal to which countless ages of existence have progressed.

At the best, man spends four-score years and ten in this world—a short time indeed!

Does a man cease to exist when he leaves the body? If his life comes to an end, then all the previous evolution is useless, all has been for nothing! Can one imagine that Creation has no greater aim than this?

The soul is eternal, immortal.

Materialists say, "Where is the soul? What is it? We cannot see it, neither can we touch it."

This is how we must answer them: However much the mineral may progress, it cannot comprehend the vegetable world. Now, that lack of comprehension does not prove the non-existence of the plant!

To however great a degree the plant may have evolved, it is unable to understand the animal world; this ignorance is no proof that the animal does not exist!

The animal, be he never so highly developed, cannot imagine the intelligence of man, neither can he realize the nature of his soul. But, again, this does not prove that man is without intellect, or without soul. It only demonstrates this, that one form of existence is incapable of comprehending a form superior to itself.

This flower may be unconscious of such a being as man, but the fact of its ignorance does not prevent the existence of humanity.

In the same way, if materialists do not believe in the existence of the soul, their unbelief does not prove that there is no such realm as the world of spirit. The very existence of man's intelligence proves his immortality; moreover, darkness proves the presence of light, for without light there would be no shadow. Poverty proves the existence of riches, for, without riches, how could we measure poverty? Ignorance proves that knowledge exists, for without knowledge how could there be ignorance?

Therefore the idea of mortality presupposes the existence of immortality—for if there were no Life Eternal, there would be no way of measuring the life of this world!

If the spirit were not immortal, how could the Manifestations of God endure such terrible trials?

Why did Christ Jesus suffer the fearful death on the cross?

Why did Muhammad bear persecutions?

Why did the Báb make the supreme sacrifice and why did Bahá'u'lláh pass the years of His life in prison?

Why should all this suffering have been, if not to prove the everlasting life of the spirit?

Christ suffered, He accepted all His trials because of the immortality of His spirit. If a man reflects he will understand the spiritual significance of the law of progress; how all moves from the inferior to the superior degree.

It is only a man without intelligence who, after considering these things, can imagine that the great scheme of creation should suddenly cease to progress, that evolution should come to such an inadequate end!

Materialists who reason in this way, and contend that we are unable to *see* the world of spirit, or to perceive the blessings of God, are surely like the animals who have no understanding; having eyes they see not, ears they have, but do not hear. And this lack of sight and hearing is a proof of nothing but their own inferiority; of whom we read in the Qur'án, "They are men who are blind and deaf to the Spirit." They do not use that great gift of God, the power of the understanding, by which they might see with the eyes of the spirit, hear with spiritual ears and also comprehend with a Divinely enlightened heart.

The inability of the materialistic mind to grasp the idea of the Life Eternal is no proof of the non-existence of that life.

The comprehension of that other life depends on our spiritual birth!

My prayer for you is that your spiritual faculties and aspirations may daily increase, and that you will never allow the material senses to veil from your eyes the glories of the Heavenly Illumination.

48

*E*very composition is necessarily subject to destruction or disintegration. For instance, this flower is a composition of various elements; its decomposition is inevitable. When this composed form undergoes decomposition—in other words, when these elements separate and disintegrate—that is what we call the death of the flower. For inasmuch as it is composed of single elements, the grouping of multitudinous cellular atoms, it is subject to disintegration. This is the mortality of the flower. Similarly, the body of man is composed of various elements. This composition of the elements has been given life. When these elements disintegrate, life disappears, and that is death. Existence in the various planes, or kingdoms, implies composition; and nonexistence, or death, is decomposition.

But the inner and essential reality of man is not

composed of elements and, therefore, cannot be decomposed. It is not an elemental composition subject to disintegration or death. A true and fundamental scientific principle is that an element itself never dies and cannot be destroyed for the reason that it is single and not composed. Therefore, it is not subject to decomposition.

Another evidence or proof of the indestructibility of the reality of man is that it is not affected by the changes of the physical body. These changing conditions of the bodily composition are definite and continual. At one time it is normal, at another time abnormal. Now it is weak, now strong. It suffers injury, a hand may be amputated, a limb broken, an eye destroyed, an ear deafened or some defect appear in a certain organ, but these changes do not affect the human spirit, the soul of man. If the body becomes stout or thin, decrepit or strong, the spirit or soul is unaffected thereby. If a part of the bodily organism be destroyed, even if it be dismembered completely, the soul continues to function, showing that no changes of the body affect its operation. We have seen that death and mortality are synonymous with change and disintegration. As we find the soul unaffected by this change and disintegration of the body, we, therefore, prove it to be immortal; for that which is changeable is accidental, evanescent.

Furthermore, this immortal human soul is endowed with two means of perception: One is effected through instrumentality; the other, independently. For instance, the soul sees through the instrumentality of the eye, hears with the ear, smells through the nostrils and grasps objects with the hands. These are the actions or operations of the soul through instruments. But in the world of dreams the soul sees when the eyes are closed. The man is seemingly dead, lies there as dead; the ears do not hear, yet he hears. The body lies there, but he—that is, the soul—travels, sees, observes. All the instruments of the body are inactive, all the functions seemingly useless. Notwithstanding this, there is an immediate and vivid perception by the soul. Exhilaration is experienced. The soul journeys, perceives, senses. It often happens that a man in a state of wakefulness has not been able to accomplish the solution of a problem, and when he goes to sleep, he will reach that solution in a dream. How often it has happened that he has dreamed, even as the prophets have dreamed, of the future; and events which have thus been foreshadowed have come to pass literally.

Therefore, we learn that the immortality of the soul, or spirit, is not contingent or dependent upon the so-called immortality of the body, because the body in the quiescent state, in the time of sleep, may be as dead, unconscious, senseless; but the soul, or spirit, is possessed of perceptions, sensations, motion and discovery. Even inspiration and revelation are obtained by it. How many were the prophets who have had marvelous visions of the future while in that state! The spirit, or human soul, is the rider; and the body is only the steed. If anything affects the steed, the rider is not affected by it. The spirit may be likened to the light within the lantern. The body is simply the outer lantern. If the lantern should break, the light is ever the same because the light could shine even without the lantern. The spirit can conduct its affairs without the body. In the world of dreams it is precisely as this light without the chimney glass. It can shine without the glass. The human soul by means of this body can perform its operations, and without the body it can, likewise, have its control. Therefore, if the body be subject to disintegration, the spirit is not affected by these changes or transformations.

It is an evident fact that the body does not conduct the process of intellection or thought radiation. It is only the medium of the grossest sensations. This human body is purely animal in type and, like the animal, it is subject only to the grosser sensibilities. It is utterly bereft of ideation or intellection, utterly incapable of the processes of reason. The animal perceives what its eye sees and judges what the ear hears. It perceives according to its animal senses, the scent of the nostril, the taste of the tongue. It comprehends not beyond its sense perceptions. The animal is confined to its feelings and sensibilities, a prisoner of the senses. Beyond these, in the finer higher processes of reasoning, the animal cannot go. For instance, the animal cannot conceive of the earth whereon it stands as a spherical object because the spherical shape of the earth is a matter of conscious reasoning. It is not a matter of sense perception. An animal in Europe could not foresee and plan the discovery of America as Columbus did. It could not take the globe map of the earth and scan the various continents, saying, "This is the eastern hemisphere; there must be another, the western hemisphere." No animal could know these things for the reason that they are referable to intellection. The animal cannot become aware of the fact that the earth is revolving and the sun stationary. Only processes of reasoning can come to this conclusion. The outward eye sees the sun as revolving. It mistakes the stars and the planets as moving about the earth. But reason decides their orbit, knows that the earth is moving and the other worlds fixed, knows that the sun is the solar center and ever occupies the same place, proves that it is the earth which revolves around it. Such conclusions are entirely intellectual, not according to the senses.

Hence, we know that in the human organism there is a center of intellection, a power of intellectual operation which is the discoverer of the realities of things. This power can unravel the mysteries of phenomena. It can comprehend that which is knowable, not alone the sensible. All the inventions are its products. For all of these have been the mysteries of nature. There was a time when the energy of electricity was a mystery of nature, but that collective reality which is manifest in man discovered this mystery of nature, this latent force. Having discovered it, man brought it into the plane of visibility. All the sciences which we now utilize are the products of that wondrous reality. But the animal is deprived of its operations. The arts we now enjoy are the expressions of that marvelous reality. The animal is bereft of them because these conscious realities are peculiar to the human spirit. All the traces are the outcoming of the perfections which comprehend realities. The animal is bereft of these.

Such evidences prove conclusively that man is possessed of two realities, as it were: a reality connected with the senses which is shared in common with the animal, and another reality which is conscious and ideal in character. This latter is the collective reality and the discoverer of mysteries. That which discovers the realities of things undoubtedly is not of the elemental substances. It is distinct from them. For mortality and disintegration are the properties inherent in compositions and are referable to things which are subject to sense perceptions, but the collective reality in man, not being so subject, is the discoverer of things. Therefore, it is real, eternal and does not have to undergo changes and transformations.

There are many other proofs concerning this vital subject, but I shall conclude with the words of Jesus Christ: "That which is born of the Spirit is spirit" and is acceptable in the Kingdom of God. This means that just as in the first birth the fetus comes forth from the matrix of the mother into the conditions of the human kingdom, even so the spirit of man must be born out of the matrix of naturalism, out of the baser nature, in order that he may comprehend the great things of the Kingdom of God. He must be born out of mother earth to find the everlasting life. And this collective reality, or spirit, of man, being born out of the world of nature, possessing the attributes of God, will continue to live forever in the eternal realm.

Appendix 1:
The Divine Educators

1

The Prophets and Messengers of God have been sent down for the sole purpose of guiding mankind to the straight Path of Truth. The purpose underlying Their revelation hath been to educate all men, that they may, at the hour of death, ascend, in the utmost purity and sanctity and with absolute detachment, to the throne of the Most High. The light which these souls radiate is responsible for the progress of the world and the advancement of its peoples. They are like unto leaven which leaveneth the world of being, and constitute the animating force through which the arts and wonders of the world are made manifest. Through them the clouds rain their bounty upon men, and the earth bringeth forth its fruits. All things must needs have a cause, a motive power, an animating principle. These souls and symbols of detachment have provided, and will continue to provide, the supreme moving impulse in the world of being.

2

He [God] hath in every age and cycle, in conformity with His transcendent wisdom, sent forth a divine Messenger to revive the dispirited and despondent souls with the living waters of His utterance, One Who is indeed the Expounder, the true Interpreter, inasmuch as man is unable to comprehend that which hath streamed forth from the Pen of Glory and is recorded in His heavenly Books. Men at all times and under all conditions stand in need of one to exhort them, guide them and to instruct and teach them. Therefore He hath sent forth His Messengers, His Prophets and chosen ones that they might acquaint the people with the divine purpose underlying the revelation of Books and the raising up of Messengers, and that everyone may become aware of the trust of God which is latent in the reality of every soul.

Man is the supreme Talisman. Lack of a proper education hath, however, deprived him of that which he doth inherently possess. Through a word proceeding out of the mouth of God he was called into being; by one word more he was guided to recognize the Source of his education; by yet another word his station and destiny were safeguarded. The Great Being saith: Regard man as a mine rich in gems of inestimable value. Education can, alone, cause it to reveal its treasures, and enable mankind to benefit therefrom.

3

*T*he greatest power in the realm and range of human existence is spirit—the divine breath which animates and pervades all things. It is manifested throughout creation in different degrees or kingdoms. In the vegetable kingdom it is the augmentative spirit or power of growth, the animus of life and development in plants, trees and organisms of the floral world. In this degree of its manifestation spirit is unconscious of the powers which qualify the kingdom of the animal. The distinctive virtue or plus of the animal is sense perception; it sees, hears, smells, tastes and feels but is incapable, in turn, of conscious ideation or reflection which characterizes and differentiates the human kingdom. The animal neither exercises nor apprehends this distinctive human power and gift. From the visible it cannot draw conclusions regarding the invisible, whereas the human mind from visible and known premises attains knowledge of the unknown and invisible. For instance, Christopher Columbus from information based upon known and provable facts drew conclusions which led him unerringly across the vast ocean to the unknown continent of America. Such power of accomplishment is beyond the range of animal intelligence. Therefore, this power is a distinctive attribute of the human spirit and kingdom. The animal spirit cannot penetrate and discover the mysteries of things. It is a captive of the senses. No amount of teaching, for instance, would enable it to grasp the fact that the sun is stationary, and the earth moves around it. Likewise, the human spirit has its limitations. It cannot comprehend the phenomena of the Kingdom transcending the human station, for it is a captive of powers and life forces which have their operation upon its own plane of existence, and it cannot go beyond that boundary.

There is, however, another Spirit, which may be termed the Divine, to which Jesus Christ refers when He declares that man must be born of its quickening and baptized with its living fire. Souls deprived of that Spirit are accounted as dead, though they are possessed of the human spirit. Jesus Christ has pronounced them dead inasmuch as they have no portion of the Divine Spirit. He says, "Let the dead bury their dead." In another instance He declares,

"That which is born of the flesh is flesh; and that which is born of the Spirit is spirit." By this He means that souls, though alive in the human kingdom, are nevertheless dead if devoid of this particular spirit of divine quickening. They have not partaken of the divine life of the higher Kingdom, for the soul which partakes of the power of the Divine Spirit is, verily, living.

This quickening spirit emanates spontaneously from the Sun of Truth, from the reality of Divinity, and is not a revelation or a manifestation. It is like the rays of the sun. The rays are emanations from the sun. This does not mean that the sun has become divisible, that a part of the sun has come out into space. This plant beside me has risen from the seed; therefore, it is a manifestation and unfoldment of the seed. The seed, as you can see, has unfolded in manifestation, and the result is this plant. Every leaf of the plant is a part of the seed. But the reality of Divinity is indivisible, and each individual of humankind cannot be a part of it as is often claimed. Nay, rather, the individual realities of mankind, when spiritually born, are emanations from the reality of Divinity, just as the flame, heat and light of the sun are the effulgence of the sun and not a part of the sun itself. Therefore, a spirit has emanated from the reality of Divinity, and its effulgences have become visible in human entities or realities. This ray and this heat are permanent. There is no cessation in the effulgence. As long as the sun exists, the heat and light will exist, and inasmuch as eternality is a property of Divinity, this emanation is everlasting. There is no cessation in its outpouring. The more the world of humanity develops, the more the effulgences or emanations of Divinity will become revealed, just as the stone, when it becomes polished and pure as a mirror, will reflect in fuller degree the glory and splendor of the sun.

The mission of the Prophets, the revelation of the Holy Books, the manifestation of the heavenly Teachers and the purpose of divine philosophy all center in the training of the human realities so that they may become clear and pure as mirrors and reflect the light and love of the Sun of Reality. Therefore, I hope that—whether you be in the East or the West—you will strive with heart and soul in order that day by day the world of humanity may become glorified, more spiritual, more sanctified; and that the splendor of the Sun of Reality may be revealed fully in human hearts as in a mirror. This is worthy of the world of mankind. This is the true evolution and progress of humanity. This is the supreme bestowal. Otherwise, by simple development along material lines man is not perfected. At most, the physical aspect of man, his natural or material conditions, may become stabilized and improved, but he will remain deprived of the spiritual or divine bestowal. He is then like a body without a spirit, a lamp without the light, an eye without the power of vision, an ear that hears no sound, a mind incapable of perceiving, an intellect minus the power of reason.

Man has two powers; and his development, two aspects. One power is connected with the material world, and by it he is capable of material advancement. The other power is spiritual, and through its development his inner, potential nature is awakened. These powers are like two wings. Both must be developed, for flight is impossible with one wing. Praise be to God! Material advancement has been evident in the world, but there is need of spiritual advancement in like proportion. We must strive unceasingly and without rest to accomplish the development of the spiritual nature in man, and endeavor with tireless energy to advance humanity toward the nobility of its true and intended station. For the body of man is accidental; it is of no importance. The time of its disintegration will inevitably come. But the spirit of man is essential and, therefore, eternal. It is a divine bounty. It is the effulgence of the Sun of Reality and, therefore, of greater importance than the physical body.

4

The spirit of man must acquire its bounties from the Kingdom of God in order that it may become the mirror and manifestation of lights and the dawning point of divine traces, because the human reality is like the soil. If no bounty of rain descends from heaven upon the soil, if no heat of the sun penetrates, it will remain black, forbidding, unproductive; but when the moistening shower and the effulgent glow of the sun's rays fall upon it, beautiful and redolent flowers grow from its bosom. Similarly, the human spirit or reality of man, unless it becomes the recipient of the lights of the Kingdom, develops divine susceptibilities and consciously reflects the effulgence of God, will not be the manifestation of ideal bounties, for only the reality of man can become the mirror wherein the lights of God are revealed. The reality of man will then be as the spirit of this world, for just as the animus of life quickens the physical human body, so the body of the world will receive its vivification through the animating virtue of the sanctified spirit of man.

It is evident that the holy Manifestations* and divine dawning points are necessary, for these blessed and glorious Souls are the foremost Teachers and Educators of mankind, and all human souls are developed through Them by the bounty of the Holy Spirit of God.

---

* Prophets, or Messengers of God.

5

God sent His Prophets into the world to teach and enlighten man, to explain to him the mystery of the power of the Holy Spirit, to enable him to reflect the light, and so in his turn, to be the source of guidance to others. The Heavenly Books, the Bible, the Qur'án, and the other Holy Writings have been given by God as guides into the paths of Divine virtue, love, justice and peace.

Therefore I say unto you that ye should strive to follow the counsels of these Blessed Books, and so order your lives that ye may, following the examples set before you, become yourselves the saints of the Most High!

6

*M*an is said to be the greatest representative of God, and he is the Book of Creation because all the mysteries of beings exist in him. If he comes under the shadow of the True Educator and is rightly trained, he becomes the essence of essences, the light of lights, the spirit of spirits; he becomes the center of the divine appearances, the source of spiritual qualities, the rising-place of heavenly lights, and the receptacle of divine inspirations. If he is deprived of this education, he becomes the manifestation of satanic qualities, the sum of animal vices, and the source of all dark conditions.

The reason of the mission of the Prophets is to educate men, so that this piece of coal may become a diamond, and this fruitless tree may be engrafted and yield the sweetest, most delicious fruits. When man reaches the noblest state in the world of humanity, then he can make further progress in the conditions of perfection, but not in state; for such states are limited, but the divine perfections are endless.

Both before and after putting off this material form, there is progress in perfection but not in state. So beings are consummated in perfect man. There is no other being higher than a perfect man. But man when he has reached this state can still make progress in perfections but not in state because there is no state higher than that of a perfect man to which he can transfer himself. He only progresses in the state of humanity, for the human perfections are infinite. Thus, however learned a man may be, we can imagine one more learned.

Hence, as the perfections of humanity are endless, man can also make progress in perfections after leaving this world.

7

*T*he Divine Reality is Unthinkable, Limitless, Eternal, Immortal and Invisible.

The world of creation is bound by natural law, finite and mortal.

The Infinite Reality cannot be said to ascend or descend. It is beyond the understanding of man, and cannot be described in terms which apply to the phenomenal sphere of the created world.

Man, then, is in extreme need of the only Power by which he is able to receive help from the Divine Reality, that Power alone bringing him into contact with the Source of all life.

An intermediary is needed to bring two extremes into relation with each other. Riches and poverty, plenty and need: without an intermediary power there could be no relation between these pairs of opposites.

So we can say there must be a Mediator between God and Man, and this is none other than the Holy Spirit, which brings the created earth into relation with the "Unthinkable One," the Divine Reality.

The Divine Reality may be likened to the sun and the Holy Spirit to the rays of the sun. As the rays of the sun bring the light and warmth of the sun to the earth, giving life to all created beings, so do the "Manifestations"* bring the power of the Holy Spirit from the Divine Sun of Reality to give light and life to the souls of men.

Behold, there is an intermediary necessary between the sun and the earth; the sun does not descend to the earth, neither does the earth ascend to the sun. This contact is made by the rays of the sun which bring light and warmth and heat.

The Holy Spirit is the Light from the Sun of Truth bringing, by its infinite power, life and illumination to all mankind, flooding all souls with Divine Radiance, conveying the blessings of God's Mercy to the whole world. The earth, without the medium of the warmth and light of the rays of the sun, could receive no benefits from the sun.

Likewise the Holy Spirit is the very cause of the life of man; without the Holy Spirit he would have

---

* Manifestations of God.

no intellect, he would be unable to acquire his scientific knowledge by which his great influence over the rest of creation is gained. The illumination of the Holy Spirit gives to man the power of thought, and enables him to make discoveries by which he bends the laws of nature to his will.

The Holy Spirit it is which, through the mediation of the Prophets of God, teaches spiritual virtues to man and enables him to attain Eternal Life.

All these blessings are brought to man by the Holy Spirit; therefore we can understand that the Holy Spirit is the Intermediary between the Creator and the created. The light and heat of the sun cause the earth to be fruitful, and create life in all things that grow; and the Holy Spirit quickens the souls of men.

Appendix 2:
The Oneness of the
Prophets of God

1

*K*now thou that they who are truly wise have likened the world unto the human temple. As the body of man needeth a garment to clothe it, so the body of mankind must needs be adorned with the mantle of justice and wisdom. Its robe is the Revelation vouchsafed unto it by God. Whenever this robe hath fulfilled its purpose, the Almighty will assuredly renew it. For every age requireth a fresh measure of the light of God. Every Divine Revelation hath been sent down in a manner that befitted the circumstances of the age in which it hath appeared.

2

*K*now thou assuredly that the essence of all the Prophets of God is one and the same. Their unity is absolute. God, the Creator, saith: There is no distinction whatsoever among the Bearers of My Message. They all have but one purpose; their secret is the same secret. To prefer one in honor to another, to exalt certain ones above the rest, is in no wise to be permitted. Every true Prophet hath regarded His Message as fundamentally the same as the Revelation of every other Prophet gone before Him. If any man, therefore, should fail to comprehend this truth, and should consequently indulge in vain and unseemly language, no one whose sight is keen and whose understanding is enlightened would ever allow such idle talk to cause him to waver in his belief.

The measure of the revelation of the Prophets of God in this world, however, must differ. Each and every one of them hath been the Bearer of a distinct Message, and hath been commissioned to reveal Himself through specific acts. It is for this reason that they appear to vary in their greatness. Their Revelation may be likened unto the light of the moon that sheddeth its radiance upon the earth. Though every time it appeareth, it revealeth a fresh measure of its brightness, yet its inherent splendor can never diminish, nor can its light suffer extinction.

It is clear and evident, therefore, that any apparent variation in the intensity of their light is not inherent in the light itself, but should rather be attributed to the varying receptivity of an ever-changing world. Every Prophet Whom the Almighty and Peerless Creator hath purposed to send to the peoples of the earth hath been entrusted with a Message, and charged to act in a manner that would best meet the requirements of the age in which He appeared. God's purpose in sending His Prophets unto men is twofold.

The first is to liberate the children of men from the darkness of ignorance, and guide them to the light of true understanding. The second is to ensure the peace and tranquillity of mankind, and provide all the means by which they can be established.

The Prophets of God should be regarded as physicians whose task is to foster the well-being of the world and its peoples, that, through the spirit of oneness, they may heal the sickness of a divided humanity. To none is given the right to question their words or disparage their conduct, for they are the only ones who can claim to have understood the patient and to have correctly diagnosed its ailments. No man, however acute his perception, can ever hope to reach the heights which the wisdom and understanding of the Divine Physician have attained. Little wonder, then, if the treatment prescribed by the physician in this day should not be found to be identical with that which he prescribed before. How could it be otherwise when the ills affecting the sufferer necessitate at every stage of his sickness a special remedy? In like manner, every time the Prophets of God have illumined the world with the resplendent radiance of the Day Star of Divine knowledge, they have invariably summoned its peoples to embrace the light of God through such means as best befitted the exigencies of the age in which they appeared. They were thus able to scatter the darkness of ignorance, and to shed upon the world the glory of their own knowledge. It is towards the inmost essence of these Prophets, therefore, that the eye of every man of discernment must be directed, inasmuch as their one and only purpose hath always been to guide the erring, and give peace to the afflicted. . . . These are not days of prosperity and triumph. The whole of mankind is in the grip of manifold ills. Strive, therefore, to save its life through the wholesome medicine which the almighty hand of the unerring Physician hath prepared.

3

*I*t is a self-evident fact that phenomenal existence can never grasp nor comprehend the ancient and essential Reality. Utter weakness cannot understand absolute strength. When we view the world of creation, we discover differences in degree which make it impossible for the lower to comprehend the higher. For example, the mineral kingdom, no matter how much it may advance, can never comprehend the phenomena of the vegetable kingdom. Whatever development the vegetable may attain, it can have no message from nor come in touch with the kingdom of the animal. However perfect may be the growth of a tree, it cannot realize the sensation of sight, hearing, smell, taste and touch; these are beyond its limitation. Although it is the possessor of existence in the world of creation, a tree, nevertheless, has no knowledge of the superior degree of the animal kingdom. Likewise, no matter how great the advancement of the animal, it can have no idea of the human plane, no knowledge of intellect and spirit. Difference in degree is an obstacle to this comprehension. A lower degree cannot comprehend a higher although all are in the same world of creation—whether mineral, vegetable or animal. Degree is the barrier and limitation. In the human plane of existence we can say we have knowledge of a vegetable, its qualities and product; but the vegetable has no knowledge or comprehension whatever of us. No matter how near perfection this rose may advance in its own sphere, it can never possess hearing and sight. Inasmuch as in the creational world, which is phenomenal, difference of degree is an obstacle or hindrance to comprehension, how can the human being, which is a created exigency, comprehend the ancient divine Reality, which is essential? This is impossible because the reality of Divinity is sanctified beyond the comprehension of the created being, man.

Furthermore, that which man can grasp is finite to man, and man to it is as infinite. Is it possible then for the reality of Divinity to be finite and the human creature infinite? On the contrary, the reverse is true; the human is finite while the essence of Divinity is infinite. Whatever comes within the sphere of human comprehension must be limited and finite. As the essence of Divinity transcends the comprehension of man, therefore God brings forth certain Manifestations of the divine Reality upon Whom He bestows heavenly effulgences in order that They may be intermediaries between humanity and Himself. These holy Manifestations or Prophets of God are as mirrors which have acquired illumination from the Sun of Truth, but the Sun does not descend from its high zenith and does not effect entrance within the mirror. In truth, this mirror has attained complete polish and purity until the utmost capacity of reflection has been developed in it; therefore, the Sun of Reality with its fullest effulgence and splendor is revealed therein. These mirrors are earthly, whereas the reality of Divinity is in its highest apogee. Although its lights are shining and its heat is manifest in them, although these mirrors are telling their story of its effulgence, the Sun, nevertheless, remains in its own lofty station; it does not descend; it does not effect entrance, because it is holy and sanctified.

The Sun of Divinity and of Reality has revealed itself in various mirrors. Though these mirrors are many, yet the Sun is one. The bestowals of God are one; the reality of the divine religion is one. Consider how one and the same light has reflected itself in the different mirrors or manifestations of it. There are certain souls who are lovers of the Sun; they perceive the effulgence of the Sun from every mirror. They are not fettered or attached to the mirrors; they are attached to the Sun itself and adore it, no matter from what point it may shine. But those who adore the mirror and are attached to it become deprived of witnessing the light of the Sun when it shines forth from another mirror. For instance, the Sun of Reality revealed itself from the Mosaic mirror. The people who were sincere accepted and believed in it. When the same Sun shone from the Messianic mirror, the Jews who were not lovers of the Sun and who were fettered by their adoration of the mirror of Moses did not perceive the lights and effulgences of the Sun of Reality resplendent in Jesus; therefore, they were deprived of its bestowals. Yet the Sun of Reality, the Word of God, shone from the Messianic mirror through the wonderful channel of Jesus Christ more fully and more wonderfully. Its effulgences were manifestly radiant, but even to this day the Jews are holding to the Mosaic mirror. Therefore, they are bereft of witnessing the lights of eternity in Jesus.

In brief, the sun is one sun, the light is one light which shines upon all phenomenal beings. Every creature has a portion thereof, but the pure mirror can reveal the story of its bounty more fully and completely. Therefore, we must adore the light of the Sun, no matter through what mirror it may be revealed. We must not entertain prejudice, for prejudice is an obstacle to realization. Inasmuch as the effulgence is one effulgence, the human realities must all become recipients of the same light, recognizing in it the compelling force that unites them in its illumination.

As this is the radiant century, it is my hope that the Sun of Truth may illumine all humanity. May the eyes be opened and the ears become attentive; may souls become resuscitated and consort together in the utmost harmony as recipients of the same light.

References

God's Love for Humanity

1. *The Hidden Words*, Arabic, no. 3.
2. *The Hidden Words*, Arabic, no. 4.
3. *The Hidden Words*, Arabic, no. 19.
4. *The Hidden Words*, Arabic, no. 5.

Relationship with God: Our Purpose in Life

5. *Gleanings from the Writings of Bahá'u'lláh,* p. 77.
6. *Gleanings from the Writings of Bahá'u'lláh,* p. 70.
7. *Gleanings from the Writings of Bahá'u'lláh,* p. 65.
8. Prayer: *Bahá'í Prayers,* p. 4.

Our Spiritual Reality

9. *Gleanings from the Writings of Bahá'u'lláh,* pp. 158–59.
10. *Gleanings from the Writings of Bahá'u'lláh,* p. 160.
11. *Paris Talks*, nos. 28.6–8.
12. *Paris Talks*, no. 2.1.

The Nature of the Soul

13. *Summons of the Lord of Hosts,* Súriy-i-Ra'ís, ¶31–34.
14. *Gleanings from the Writings of Bahá'u'lláh,* pp. 164–66.
15. *Summons of the Lord of Hosts,* Súriy-i-Ra'ís, ¶35.
16. *Paris Talks,* nos. 31.1–5.
17. *Paris Talks,* nos. 18.2–5.
18. *Some Answered Questions,* pp. 151–52.
19. *Paris Talks,* nos. 28.13–17.
20. *Paris Talks,* nos. 20.2–11.

Spiritual Development

21. *Gleanings from the Writings of Bahá'u'lláh,* p. 149.
22. *Selections from the Writings of Abdu'l-Bahá,* no. 159.2.
23. *The Promulgation of Universal Peace,* pp. 225–26.
24. *The Promulgation of Universal Peace,* pp. 226–27.
25. *The Promulgation of Universal Peace,* pp. 451–52.
26. *The Promulgation of Universal Peace,* pp. 90–91.
27. *The Promulgation of Universal Peace,* pp. 147–48.
28. *Paris Talks,* no. 20.15.
29. *The Promulgation of Universal Peace,* pp. 148–49.
30. *Paris Talks,* nos. 29.2–11.
31. *Paris Talks,* nos. 31.6–10.
32. *The Promulgation of Universal Peace,* pp. 302–05.
33. *The Promulgation of Universal Peace,* pp. 294–96.
34. *The Promulgation of Universal Peace,* pp. 89–90.
35. *Some Answered Questions,* p. 228.

Immortality and Life Hereafter

36. *The Promulgation of Universal Peace,* p. 88.
37. *The Promulgation of Universal Peace,* p. 47.
38. *'Abdu'l-Bahá in London,* pp. 95–96.
39. *Gleanings from the Writings of Bahá'u'lláh,* p. 161.
40. *Gleanings from the Writings of Bahá'u'lláh,* pp. 155–56.
41. *Gleanings from the Writings of Bahá'u'lláh,* p. 125.
42. *The Hidden Words,* Arabic, no. 31.
43. *Gleanings from the Writings of Bahá'u'lláh,* pp. 156, 157–58.
44. *Gleanings from the Writings of Bahá'u'lláh,* p. 171.
45. *Gleanings from the Writings of Bahá'u'lláh,* pp. 153–55.
46. *Paris Talks,* nos. 20.12–15.
47. *Paris Talks,* nos. 29.12–41.
48. *The Promulgation of Universal Peace,* pp. 415–18.

Appendix 1: The Divine Educators

1. *Gleanings from the Writings of Bahá'u'lláh,* pp. 156–57.
2. *Tablets of Bahá'u'lláh,* pp. 161–62.
3. *The Promulgation of Universal Peace,* pp. 58–60.
4. *The Promulgation of Universal Peace,* pp. 330–31.
5. *Paris Talks,* nos. 18.6–7.
6. *Some Answered Questions,* pp. 236–37.
7. *Paris Talks,* nos. 17.1–13.

Appendix 2:
The Oneness of the Prophets of God

1. *Gleanings from the Writings of Bahá'u'lláh,* p. 81.
2. *Gleanings from the Writings of Bahá'u'lláh,* pp. 78–81.
3. *The Promulgation of Universal Peace,* pp. 113–15.

Bibliography

Works of Bahá'u'lláh

Gleanings from the Writings of Bahá'u'lláh. 1st pocket-size ed. Translated by Shoghi Effendi. Wilmette, IL: Bahá'í Publishing Trust, 1983.

The Hidden Words. Translated by Shoghi Effendi. Wilmette, IL: Bahá'í Publishing, 2002.

The Summons of the Lord of Hosts: Tablets of Bahá'u'lláh. Haifa, Israel: Bahá'í World Centre, 2002.

Tablets of Bahá'u'lláh revealed after the Kitáb-i-Aqdas. Compiled by the Research Department of the Universal House of Justice. Translated by Habib Taherzadeh et al. Wilmette, IL: Bahá'í Publishing Trust, 1988.

Works of 'Abdu'l-Bahá

'Abdu'l-Bahá in London: Addresses and Notes of Conversations. [Compiled by Eric Hammond.] London: Longmans Green, 1912; reprinted Bahá'í Publishing Trust, 1982.

Paris Talks: Addresses Given by 'Abdu'l-Bahá in Paris in 1911. 12th ed. London: Bahá'í Publishing Trust, 1995.

The Promulgation of Universal Peace: Talks Delivered by 'Abdu'l-Bahá during His Visit to the United States and Canada in 1912. Compiled by Howard MacNutt. 2d ed. Wilmette, IL: Bahá'í Publishing Trust, 1982.

Selections from the Writings of 'Abdu'l-Bahá. Compiled by the Research Department of the Universal House of Justice. Translated by a Committee at the Bahá'í World Center and Marzieh Gail. Wilmette, IL: Bahá'í Publishing Trust, 1997.

Some Answered Questions. Compiled and translated by Laura Clifford Barney. 1st pocket-size ed. Wilmette, IL: Bahá'í Publishing Trust, 1984.

Compilations

Bahá'u'lláh, the Báb, and 'Abdu'l-Bahá. *Bahá'í Prayers: A Selection of Prayers Revealed by Bahá'u'lláh, the Báb, and 'Abdu'l-Bahá.* Wilmette, IL: Bahá'í Publishing Trust, 2002.

A Basic Bahá'í Reading List

The following list provides a sampling of works conveying the spiritual truths, social principles, and history of the Bahá'í Faith.

Introductory Works

Bahá'í International Community, Office of Public Information, New York. *Bahá'u'lláh*. Wilmette, IL: Bahá'í Publishing Trust, 1991.

Bowers, Kenneth E. *God Speaks Again: An Introduction to the Bahá'í Faith*. Wilmette, IL: Bahá'í Publishing, 2004.

Hatcher, William S., and J. Douglas Martin. *The Bahá'í Faith: The Emerging Global Religion*. Wilmette, IL: Bahá'í Publishing, 2002.

Smith, Peter. *A Concise Encyclopedia of the Bahá'í Faith*. Oxford: Oneworld Publications, 2000.

Selected Writings of Bahá'u'lláh

Gleanings from the Writings of Bahá'u'lláh. 1st ps ed. Translated by Shoghi Effendi. Wilmette, IL: Bahá'í Publishing Trust, 1983.

The Hidden Words. Translated by Shoghi Effendi. Wilmette, IL: Bahá'í Publishing, 2002.

The Kitáb-i-Aqdas: The Most Holy Book. Wilmette, IL: Bahá'í Publishing Trust, 1993.

The Kitáb-i-Íqán: The Book of Certitude. 1st ps ed. Translated by Shoghi Effendi. Wilmette, IL: Bahá'í Publishing Trust, 1983.

Tablets of Bahá'u'lláh revealed after the Kitáb-i-Aqdas. Compiled by the Research Department of the Universal House of Justice. Translated by Habib Taherzadeh. 1st ps ed. Wilmette, IL: Bahá'í Publishing Trust, 1998.

Selected Writings of 'Abdu'l-Bahá

Paris Talks: Addresses given by 'Abdu'l-Bahá in Paris in 1911. 12th ed. London: Bahá'í Publishing Trust, 1995.

The Promulgation of Universal Peace: Talks Delivered by 'Abdu'l-Bahá during His Visit to the United States and Canada in 1912. Compiled by Howard MacNutt. 2nd ed. Wilmette, IL: Bahá'í Publishing Trust, 1982.

The Secret of Divine Civilization. 1st ps ed. Translated by Marzieh Gail and Ali-Kuli Khán. Wilmette, IL: Bahá'í Publishing Trust, 1990.

Selections from the Writings of 'Abdu'l-Bahá. Compiled by the Research Department of the Universal House of Justice. Translated by a Committee at the Bahá'í World Center and Marzieh Gail. Wilmette, IL: Bahá'í Publishing Trust, 1997.

Some Answered Questions. Compiled and translated by Laura Clifford Barney. 1st ps ed. Wilmette, IL: Bahá'í Publishing Trust, 1984.

Index

For more information about the Bahá'í Faith,

or to contact the Bahá'ís near you, visit

http://www.us.bahai.org/

or call

1-800-22-UNITE

Bahá'í Publishing
and the Bahá'í Faith

Bahá'í Publishing produces books based on the teachings of the
Bahá'í Faith. Founded nearly 160 years ago, the Bahá'í Faith has
spread to some 235 nations and territories and is now accepted
by more than five million people. The word "Bahá'í" means
"follower of Bahá'u'lláh." Bahá'u'lláh, the Founder of the Bahá'í
Faith, asserted that He is the Messenger of God for all of
humanity in this day. The cornerstone of His teachings is the
establishment of the spiritual unity of humankind, which will be
achieved by personal transformation and the application of
clearly identified spiritual principles. Bahá'ís also believe that
there is but one religion and that all the Messengers of God—
among them Abraham, Zoroaster, Moses, Krishna, Buddha, Jesus,
and Muḥammad—have progressively revealed its nature.
Together, the world's great religions are expressions of a single,
unfolding divine plan. Human beings, not God's Messengers, are
the source of religious divisions, prejudices, and hatreds.

The Bahá'í Faith is not a sect or denomination of another
religion, nor is it a cult or a social movement. Rather, it is a
globally recognized independent world religion founded on
new books of scripture revealed by Bahá'u'lláh.

Bahá'í Publishing is an imprint of the National Spiritual
Assembly of the Bahá'ís of the United States.

Other Books Available from Bahá'í Publishing

The Hidden Words

by Bahá'u'lláh

A collection of lyrical, gem-like verses of scripture that convey timeless spiritual wisdom "clothed in the garment of brevity," the Hidden Words is one of the most important and cherished scriptural works of the Bahá'í Faith.

Revealed by Bahá'u'lláh, the founder of the religion, the verses are a perfect guidebook to walking a spiritual path and drawing closer to God. They address themes such as turning to God, humility, detachment, and love, to name but a few. These verses are among Bahá'u'lláh's earliest and best-known works, having been translated into more than seventy languages and read by millions worldwide. This edition will offer many American readers their first introduction to the vast collection of Bahá'í scripture.

The Kitáb-i-Íqán: The Book of Certitude

by Bahá'u'lláh

The Book of Certitude is one of the most important scriptural works in all of religious history. In it Bahá'u'lláh gives a sweeping overview of religious truth, explaining the underlying unity of the world's religions, describing the universality of the revelations humankind has received from the Prophets of God, illuminating their fundamental teachings, and elucidating allegorical passages from the New Testament and the Koran that have given rise to misunderstandings among religious leaders, practitioners, and the public. Revealed in the span of two days and two nights, the work is, in the words of its translator, Shoghi Effendi, "the most important book written on the spiritual significance" of the Bahá'í Faith.

Advancement of Women: A Bahá'í Perspective

by Janet A. Khan and Peter J. Khan

Advancement of Women presents the Bahá'í Faith's global perspective on the equality of the sexes, including:
- The meaning of equality
- The education of women and the need for their participation in the world at large
- The profound effects of equality on the family and family relationships
- The intimate relationship between equality of the sexes and global peace
- Chastity, modesty, sexual harassment, and rape

The equality of women and men is one of the basic tenets of the Bahá'í Faith, and much is said on the subject in Bahá'í writings. Until now, however, no single volume created for a general audience has provided comprehensive coverage of the Bahá'í teachings on this topic. In this broad survey, husband-

and-wife team Janet and Peter Khan address even those aspects of equality of the sexes that are usually ignored or glossed over in the existing literature.

Tactfully treating a subject that often provokes argumentation, contention, polarization of attitudes, and accusations, the authors elevate the discussion to a new level that challenges all while offending none.

The Bahá'í Faith: The Emerging Global Religion

by William S. Hatcher and J. Douglas Martin

Explore the history, teachings, structure, and community life of the worldwide Bahá'í community—what may well be the most diverse organized body of people on earth—through this revised and updated comprehensive introduction (2002).

Named by the *Encylopaedia Britannica* as a book that has made "significant contributions to knowledge and understanding" of religious thought, *The Bahá'í Faith* covers the most recent developments in a Faith that, in just over 150 years, has grown to become the second most widespread of the independent world religions.

"An excellent introduction. [*The Bahá'í Faith*] offers a clear analysis of the religious and ethical values on which Bahá'ism is based (such as all-embracing peace, world harmony, the important role of women, to mention only a few)."
—Annemarie Schimmel, past president, International Association for the History of Religions

"Provide[s] non-Bahá'í readers with an excellent introduction to the history, beliefs, and sociopolitical structure of a religion that originated in Persia in the mid-1800s and has since blossomed into an international organization with . . . adherents from almost every country on earth."—*Montreal Gazette*

The Challenge of Bahá'u'lláh:
Does God Still Speak to Humanity Today?

by Gary L. Matthews

One person examines the astonishing claims made by the
Prophet who founded the Bahá'í religion.

Author Gary Matthews documents why he believes that the
Revelation of Bahá'u'lláh is divine in origin, representing a
unique summons of unequaled importance to humanity. The
book contains discussions of Bahá'í prophecies concerning
historical events and scientific discoveries. Among the events and
discoveries discussed are the fall of the Ottoman Empire, the
worldwide erosion of ecclesiastical authority, the Holocaust, and
the development of nuclear weapons. A new and updated
edition. The previous edition (George Ronald, ISBN 0-85398-
360-7) was a limited release and not offered to the U.S. trade/
consumer market.

Close Connections: The Bridge between
Spiritual and Physical Reality

by John S. Hatcher

Examines the bonds between physical and spiritual reality and
their implications for science.

Close Connections will appeal to anyone interested in
spirituality and its link to everyday life. For more than twenty-
five years John Hatcher has studied the nature and purpose of
physical reality by exploring the theological and philosophical
implications of the authoritative Bahá'í texts. His latest book
explains how the gap between physical and spiritual reality is
routinely crossed, and describes the profound implications that
result from the interplay of both worlds.

God Speaks Again:
An Introduction to the Bahá'í Faith

by Kenneth E. Bowers

Written by an internationally known member of the Bahá'í community, *God Speaks Again* is the first comprehensive introduction to the Bahá'í Faith written for general readers that includes many important and beautiful passages of Bahá'í scripture to both illustrate and explain the Faith's history, teachings, and distinctive relevance for life on our planet today. The book contains 30 chapters covering all aspects of the religion, as well as notes, a glossary, a bibliography, and a suggested reading list. The history and teachings of the Bahá'í Faith center around the inspiring person of its Prophet and Founder, Bahá'u'lláh (1817–1892). The extraordinary qualities that Bahá'u'lláh displayed throughout the course of His life, the voluminous and comprehensive body of His written works, and the impact they continue to have around the globe undeniably qualify Him as a major figure in world religious history.

It's Not Your Fault: How Healing Relationships Change Your Brain & Can Help You Overcome a Painful Past

by Patricia Romano McGraw

Simply put, you can't think your way to happiness if you're suffering the effects of trauma or abuse. Yet every day, millions receive this message from a multi-billion-dollar self-help industry. As a result, many think it's their fault when their efforts to heal themselves fail. Far too many sincere, intelligent, and highly motivated people who have followed popular advice for self-healing still feel depressed, anxious, unloved, and unlovable.

Why is this? If popular pathways for self-healing don't work, what does? How can those who suffer begin to find relief, function better, and feel genuinely optimistic, relaxed, loved, and lovable? This engaging and highly readable book, based on the author's professional experience in treating those who suffer from the devastating effects of emotional trauma, offers hope for those who suffer and those who care about them. McGraw describes how trauma affects the brain and, therefore, one's ability to carry out "good advice"; explains the subtle and largely hidden processes of attunement and attachment that take place between parents and children, examining their impact on all future relationships; tells what is needed for healing to occur; discusses the profound health benefits of spirituality and a relationship with God in assisting and accelerating the healing process; and suggests how members of the helping professions can begin to tap the deepest, most authentic parts of themselves to touch the hearts of those they seek to help.

Marriage beyond Black and White: An Interracial Family Portrait
by David Douglas and Barbara Douglas

A powerful story about the marriage of a Black man and a White woman, *Marriage beyond Black and White* offers a poignant and sometimes painful look at what it was like to be an interracial couple in the United States from the early 1940s to the mid-1990s. Breaking one of the strongest taboos in American society at the time, Barbara Wilson Tinker and Carlyle Douglas met, fell in love, married, and began raising a family. At the time of their wedding, interracial marriage was outlawed in twenty-seven states and was regarded as an anathema in the rest.

Barbara began writing their story to record both the triumphs and hardships of interracial marriage. Her son David completed the family chronicle. The result will uplift and inspire any reader whose life is touched by injustice, offering an invaluable perspective on the roles of faith and spiritual transformation in combating prejudice and racism.

Prophet's Daughter: The Life and Legacy of Bahíyyih Khánum, Outstanding Heroine of the Bahá'í Faith

by Janet A. Khan

The first full-length biography of a member of Bahá'u'lláh's family, an important woman in world religious history.

A biography of a largely unknown yet important woman in world religious history—the eldest daughter of Bahá'u'lláh, founder of the Bahá'í religion—who faithfully served her family and the early followers of a then completely new faith through nearly seven decades of extreme hardship. During the mid-nineteenth and early twentieth centuries, when women in the Middle East were largely invisible, deprived of education, and without status in their communities, she was an active participant in the religion's turbulent early years and contributed significantly to its emergence as an independent world religion. The example of her life and her remarkable personal qualities have special relevance to issues confronting society today.

Refresh and Gladden My Spirit: Prayers and Meditations from Bahá'í Scripture

Introduction by Pamela Brode

Discover the Bahá'í approach to prayer with this uplifting collection of prayers and short, inspirational extracts from Bahá'í scripture. More than 120 prayers in *Refresh and Gladden My Spirit* offer solace and inspiration on themes including spiritual growth, nearness to God, comfort, contentment, happiness, difficult times, healing, material needs, praise and gratitude, and strength, to name only a few. An introduction by Pamela Brode examines the powerful effects of prayer and meditation in daily life, outlines the Bahá'í approach to prayer, and considers questions such as "What is prayer?" "Why pray?" "Are our prayers answered?" and "Does prayer benefit the world?"

Release the Sun

by William Sears

Millennial fervor gripped many people around the world in the early nineteenth century. While Christians anticipated the return of Jesus Christ, a wave of expectation swept through Islam that the "Lord of the Age" would soon appear. In Persia, this reached a dramatic climax on May 23, 1844, when a twenty-five-year-old merchant from Shíráz named Siyyid 'Alí-Muḥammad, later titled "the Báb," announced that he was the bearer of a divine Revelation destined to transform the spiritual life of the human race. Furthermore, he claimed that he was but the herald of another Messenger, who would soon bring a far greater Revelation that would usher in an age of universal peace. Against a backdrop of wide-scale moral decay in Persian society, this declaration aroused hope and excitement among all classes. The Báb quickly attracted tens of thousands of followers, including influential members of the clergy—and the brutal hand of a fearful government bent on destroying this movement that threatened to rock the established order.

Release the Sun tells the extraordinary story of the Báb, the Prophet-Herald of the Bahá'í Faith. Drawing on contemporary accounts, William Sears vividly describes one of the most significant but little-known periods in religious history since the rise of Christianity and Islam.

Seeking Faith: Is Religion Really What You Think It Is?

by Nathan Rutstein

What's your concept of religion? A 2001 Gallup Poll on religion in America found that while nearly two out of three Americans claim to be a member of a church or synagogue, more than half of those polled believe that religion is losing its influence on society. *Seeking Faith* examines today's concepts of religion and the various reasons why people are searching in new directions for hope and spiritual guidance. Author Nathan Rutstein explores the need for a sense of purpose, direction, and meaning in life, and the need for spiritual solutions to global problems in the social, economic, environmental, and political realms. Rutstein also discusses the concept of the Spiritual Guide, or Divine Educator, and introduces the teachings of Bahá'u'lláh and the beliefs of the Bahá'í Faith.

The Story of Bahá'u'lláh: Promised One of All Religions

by Druzelle Cederquist

An easy-to-read introduction to the Prophet and Founder of the Bahá'í Faith.

The Story of Bahá'u'lláh presents in a clear narrative style the life of the Prophet from His birth into a wealthy merchant family, through His transforming spiritual experience while incarcerated in the infamous Black Pit of Tehran, and over the decades of harsh and increasingly remote exile that followed. Woven into the story are Bahá'u'lláh's principal teachings and references to historical events and persons that place the development of the new religion in a global perspective. This book chronologically follows the story told in *Release the Sun* (Bahá'í Publishing, 2003).

As explained in such resources as *The Oxford Dictionary of World Religions* and the *Encyclopaedia Britannica*, members of the Bahá'í Faith believe that all the founders of the world's great religions have been Messengers of God and agents of a progressive divine plan for the education of the human race. According to Bahá'u'lláh (1819–1892), the Prophet and Founder of the Bahá'í religion, the teachings of the divine Messengers—including Abraham, Moses, Buddha, Christ, Muhammad—vary with the receptivity and maturity of the people of their era, but all represent one single "religion of God." Bahá'u'lláh, Whom Bahá'ís accept as the divine Messenger for the present age, taught that the unity of all the peoples of the earth is the spiritual destiny of this period in human history.

A Wayfarer's Guide to Bringing the Sacred Home

by Joseph Sheppherd

What's the spiritual connection between self, family, and community? Why is it so important that we understand and cultivate these key relationships? *A Wayfarer's Guide to Bringing the Sacred Home* offers a Bahá'í perspective on issues that shape our lives and the lives of those around us: the vital role of spirituality in personal transformation, the divine nature of child-rearing and unity in the family, and the importance of overcoming barriers to building strong communities—each offering joy, hope, and confidence to a challenged world. Inspiring extracts and prayers from Bahá'í scripture are included. This is an enlightening read for anyone seeking to bring spirituality into their daily lives.

VISIT YOUR FAVORITE BOOKSTORE TODAY
TO FIND OR REQUEST THESE TITLES
FROM BAHÁ'Í PUBLISHING.